C++

Books LLC®, Reference Series, Memphis, USA, 2011. ISBN: 9781156415351. www.booksllc.net.

Table of Contents

Introduction

Purchase of this book entitles you to a free trial membership in the publisher's book club at www.booksllc.net. (Time limited offer.) Simply enter the barcode number from the back cover onto the membership form. The book club entitles you to select from hundreds of thousands of books at no additional charge. You can also download a digital copy of this and related books to read on the go. Simply enter the title or subject onto the search form to find them.

Each chapter in this book ends with a URL to a hyperlinked online version. Type the URL exactly as it appears. If you change the URL's capitalization it won't work. Use the online version to access related pages, websites, footnotes, tables, color photos, updates. Click the version history tab to see the chapter's contributors. Click the edit link to suggest changes.

A large and diverse editor base collaboratively wrote the book, not a single author. After a long process of discussion and debate, the chapters gradually took on a neutral point of view reached through consensus. Additional editors expanded and contributed to chapters striving to achieve balance and comprehensive coverage. This reduced the regional or cultural bias found in many other books and provided access and breadth on subject matter otherwise little documented.

ACCU (organisation)

ACCU (previously known as *Association of C and C++ Users*) is a non-profit, worldwide user group of people interested in software development, dedicated to raising the standard of programming. Originally, the association was mainly for C programmers, but it has expanded over time to include all programming languages, especially C++, C#, Java, Perl and Python.

The ACCU publishes two journals and organizes a conference annually in or near Oxford.

History

ACCU was formed in 1987 by Martin Houston. The original name of the organisation was *C Users' Group (UK)* and this remains the formal name of the organisation today, although it adopted the public name *Association of C and C++ Users* for the period 1993-2006, and adopted the shorter form *ACCU* from 2006 onward. The ACCU is operated by a volunteer committee, elected at an Annual General Meeting which usually takes place during the annual ACCU conference each Spring in or near Oxford.

As the formal name suggests, the organisation was originally created for people in the United Kingdom. However, the membership is now worldwide, predominantly European and North American, but also with members from central and southern America, Australasia, Africa and Asia.

Source (edited): "http://en.wikipedia.org/wiki/ACCU_(organisation)"

Alexander Stepanov

Alexander Stepanov

Alexander Alexandrovich Stepanov (Russian: Александр Александрович Степанов) (born November 16, 1950 in Moscow) is the primary designer and implementer of the C++ Standard Template Library, which he started to develop around 1992 while employed at HP Labs. He had earlier been working for Bell Labs close to Andrew Koenig and tried to convince Bjarne Stroustrup to introduce something like Ada Generics in C++.

He is the author (with Paul McJones) of Elements of Programming, a book that grew out of a "Foundations of Programming" course that Stepanov taught at Adobe Systems (while employed there).

He is currently employed by A9.com.

Standard Template Library and generic programming

Alexander Stepanov is an advocate of what is known as generic programming. Although David Musser had developed and advocated some aspects of generic programming already by 1971, it was limited to a rather specialized area of software development (computer algebra).

Stepanov recognized the full potential for generic programming and persuaded his then-colleagues at General Electric Research and Development (including, primarily, David Musser and Deepak Kapur) that generic programming should be pursued as a comprehensive basis for software development. At the time there was no real support in any programming language for generic programming.

The first major language to provide such support was Ada, with its generic units feature. By 1987 Stepanov and Musser had developed and published an Ada library for list processing that embodied the results of much of their research on generic programming. However, Ada had not achieved much acceptance outside the defense industry and C++ seemed more likely to become widely used and provide good support for generic programming even though the language was relatively immature. Another reason for turning to C++, which Stepanov recognized early on, was the C/C++ model of computation which allows very flexible access to storage via pointers is crucial to achieving generality without losing efficiency. It eventually led to the development of the Standard Template Library of C++.

Criticism of OOP

In several interviews, Stepanov has voiced strong criticisms of OOP:

- "I think that object orientedness is almost as much of a hoax as Artificial Intelligence..."
- "I find OOP technically unsound. It attempts to decompose the world in terms of interfaces that vary on a single type. To deal with the real problems you need multisorted algebras - families of interfaces that span multiple types. I find OOP

philosophically unsound. It claims that everything is an object. Even if it is true it is not very interesting - saying that everything is an object is saying nothing at all. I find OOP methodologically wrong. It starts with classes. It is as if mathematicians would start with axioms. You do not start with axioms - you start with proofs. Only when you have found a bunch of related proofs, can you come up with axioms. You end with axioms. The same thing is true in programming: you have to start with interesting algorithms. Only when you understand them well, can you come up with an interface that will let them work."

Source (edited): "http://en.wikipedia.org/wiki/Alexander_Stepanov"

Andrei Alexandrescu

Andrei Alexandrescu is a Romanian C ++ programmer and author. He is particularly known for his pioneering work on policy-based design implemented via template metaprogramming. These ideas are articulated in his book *Modern C++ Design* and were first implemented in his programming library, Loki. He also implemented the "move constructors" concept in his MOJO library. He contributed to the *C/C++ Users Journal* under the byline "Generic<Programming>". Alexandrescu is currently a research scientist at Facebook.

Education and career

Alexandrescu received an M.S. degree in electronics from Polytechnic University of Bucharest (*Universitatea Politehnica din Bucureşti*) in July 1994.

His first article was published in the C/C++ Users Journal in September 1998. He was a program manager for Netzip, Inc. from April 1999 until February 2000. When the company was acquired by RealNetworks, Inc., he served there as a development manager from February 2000 through September 2001.

Alexandrescu earned an M.S. (2003) and a Ph.D. (2009) in computer science from the University of Washington.

More recently, he has been assisting Walter Bright in the development of the D programming language. Alexandrescu released a book titled *The D Programming Language* in May 2010.

Source (edited): "http://en.wikipedia.org/wiki/Andrei_Alexandrescu"

Argument-dependent name lookup

In the C++ programming language, **argument-dependent lookup** (**ADL**), or **argument-dependent name lookup**, applies to the lookup of an unqualified function name depending on the types of the arguments given to the function call. This behavior is also known as **Koenig lookup**, named after its inventor Andrew Koenig.

ADL only occurs if the normal lookup of an unqualified name fails to find a matching class member function. In this case, other namespaces not considered during normal lookup may be searched where the set of namespaces to be searched depends on the types of the function arguments. Specifically, the set of declarations found by lookup and considered for resolution of the function name is the union of the declarations found by normal lookup with the declarations found by looking in the set of namespaces associated with the types of the function arguments.

Type-associated namespaces

The set of associated namespaces for any type T is the structural scope of T (which can be used to locate friend functions) and the namespace where T is defined, if T is a structure type, together with the namespaces associated with the structure types necessary for defining the type T, excluding the types necessary only for defining members. This set of associated namespaces is included for resolving a function call with an argument of type T.

Example

An example of **ADL** looks like this:

```
namespace NS
{
  class A {};
  void f( A *&, int ) {}
}
int main()
{
  NS::A *a;
  f( a, 0 );    //calls NS::f
}
```

A common pattern in the C++ Standard Library is to declare overloaded operators that will be found in this manner. For example, this simple Hello World program would not compile if it weren't for **ADL**:

```
#include<iostream>

int main()
{
 std::cout << "Hello World, where did operator<<() come from?" << std::endl;
 return 0;
}
```

Using << is equivalent to calling operator<<, which however lacks the std qualifier. In this case, function std::ostream& std::operator<<(std::ostream&, const char*) is found through **ADL**.

Note that std::endl is a function but it needs full qualification, since it is used as an argument to operator<< (std::endl is a function pointer, not a function call).

Interfaces

Within C++, functions found by ADL are considered part of a class's interface.

Within the Standard Template Library, several algorithms make use of unqualified calls to swap from within the std namespace. As a result, the generic std::swap function is used if nothing else is found, but if these algorithms are used with a third-party class, Foo, found in another namespace that also contains swap(Foo&, Foo&), that overload of swap will be used.

Criticism

While ADL makes it practical for free functions to be part of the interface of a class, it makes namespaces less strict and so can require the use of fully qualified names when they would not otherwise be needed. For example, the C++ standard library makes extensive use of unqualified calls to std::swap to swap two values. The idea being that then one can define an own version of std::swap in one's own namespace and it will be used within the STL algorithms. In other words, the behavior of

```
std::swap(a, b);
```

may or may not be the same as the behavior of

```
using std::swap;
swap(a, b);
```

(where a and b are of type N::A) because if N::swap(N::A&, N::A&) exists, the second of the above examples call it while the first will not. Furthermore, if for some reason both N::swap(N::A&, N::A&) and std::swap(N::A&, N::A&) are defined, then the first example will call std::swap(N::A&, N::A&) but the second will not compile because swap(a, b) would be ambiguous.

In general, over-dependence on ADL can lead to semantic problems. If one library, L1, expects unqualified calls to foo(T) to have one meaning and another library, L2 expects it to have another, then namespaces lose their utility. If, however, L1 expects L1::foo(T) to have one meaning and L2 does likewise, then there is no conflict, but calls to foo(T) would have to be fully qualified (as opposed to using L1::foo; foo(x);) lest ADL get in the way.

Source (edited): "http://en.wikipedia.org/wiki/Argument-dependent_name_lookup"

AspectC++

AspectC++ is an aspect-oriented extension of C and C++ languages. It is based on source-to-source translation, translating AspectC++ source code to C++. It is available under the GNU GPL, though some extensions specific to Microsoft Windows are only available through pure-systems GmbH.

Aspect-oriented programming allows modularizing cross-cutting concerns in a single module, an aspect. Aspects can modify existing classes, but most commonly they provide 'advice' that runs before, after, or around existing functionality.

For example, all calls to a specific function can be traced using an aspect, rather than inserting 'cerr' or print statements in many places:

```
aspect Tracer
{
  advice call("% %Iter::Reset(...)") : before()
  {
    cerr << "about to call Iter::Reset for " << JoinPoint::signature() << endl;
  }
};
```

The Tracer aspect will print out a message before any call to %Iter::Reset. The %Iter syntax means that it will match all classes that end in Iter.

Each 'matched' location in the source code is called a join point -- the advice is joined to (or advises) that code. AspectC++ provides a join point API to provide and access to information about the join point. For example, the function:

```
JoinPoint::signature()
```

returns the name of the function (that matched %Iter::Reset) that is about to be called.

The join point API also provides compile-time type information that can be used within an aspect to access the type or the value of the arguments and the return type and return value of a method or function.

Source (edited): "http://en.wikipedia.org/wiki/AspectC%2B%2B"

Assignment operator (C++)

In the C++ programming language, the **assignment operator**, '=', is the operator used for assignment. Like most other operators in C++, it can be overloaded.

The **copy assignment operator**, often just called the "assignment operator", is a special case of assignment operator where the source (right-hand side) and destination (left-hand side) are of the same class type. It is one of the special member functions, which means that a default version of it is generated automatically by the compiler if the programmer does not declare one. The default version performs a memberwise copy, where each member is copied by its own copy assignment operator (which may also be programmer-declared or compiler-generated).

The copy assignment operator differs from the copy constructor in that it must clean up the data members of the assignment's target (and correctly handle self-assignment) whereas the copy constructor assigns values to uninitialized data members. For example:

```
My_Array first;          // initialization
by default constructor
My_Array second(first);  //
initialization by copy constructor
My_Array third = first;  // Also
initialization by copy constructor
second = third;          // assignment by
copy assignment operator
```

Overloading copy assignment operator

When deep copies of objects have to be made, exception safety should be taken into consideration. One way to achieve this when resource deallocation never fails is:

- Acquire new resources
- Release old resources
- Assign the new resources' handles to the object

```
class My_Array
{

  int * array;
  int count;

public:

  My_Array & operator= (const My
_Array & other)
  {
    if (this != &other) // protect
against invalid self-assignment
    {
      // 1: allocate new memory and
copy the elements
      int * new_array = new int[other.
count];
      std::copy(other.array, other.
array + other.count, new_array);

      // 2: deallocate old memory
      delete [] array;

      // 3: assign the new memory to
the object
      array = new_array;
      count = other.count;
    }
    // by convention, always return
*this
    return *this;
  }

  ...

};
```

However, if a no-fail (no-throw) swap function is available for all the member subobjects and the class provides a copy constructor and destructor (which it should do according to the rule of three), the most straightforward way to implement copy assignment is as follows :

```
public:

  void swap(My_Array & other) // the
swap member function (should never
fail!)
  {
    // swap all the members (and base
subobject, if applicable) with other
    std::swap(array, other.array);
    std::swap(count, other.count);
  }

  My_Array & operator = (My_Array
other) // note: argument passed by
value!
  {
    // swap this with other
    swap(other);

    // by convention, always return
*this
    return *this;

    // other is destroyed, releasing the
memory
  }
```

The reason why operator = returns My_Array& instead of void is to allow chained assignments like the following:

```
array_1 = array_2 = array_3; // array_3
is assigned to array_2
                             // and then array_2 is
assigned to array_1
```

The operator returns a non-const My_Array& to allow chained assignments:

```
(array_1 = array_2) = array_3; // array
_2 is assigned to array_1
                               // and then array_3
is assigned to array_1
```

Note that this is allowed for basic types like int.

Source (edited): "http://en.wikipedia.org/wiki/Assignment_operator_(C%2B%2B)"

Auto-linking

Auto-linking is a mechanism for automatically determining which libraries to link to while building a C or C++ program. It is activated by means of **#pragma comment(lib, <name>)** statements in the header files of the library.

Most Windows compilers support auto-linking, while GCC does not support auto-linking .

Source (edited): "http://en.wikipedia. org/wiki/Auto-linking"

BCX

BCX, a free software programming application written by Kevin Diggins, which translates BASIC source code to C/C++ source code, which can then be compiled using any of several Win32 C/C++ compilers. BCX is written in BCX BASIC, making it a self-translating translator.

Source (edited): "http://en.wikipedia. org/wiki/BCX"

Bjarne Stroustrup

Bjarne Stroustrup (Danish pronunciation: [ˈbjɑːnə ˈsdʁʌʊ̯ˀsdʁɔb], English pronunciation: /-strustrɔp/ or /-straʊstrɔp/); born December 30, 1950 in Århus, Denmark) is a Danish computer scientist, most notable for the creation and the development of the widely used C++ programming language. He is currently Professor and holder of the College of Engineering Chair in Computer Science at Texas A&M University.

Stroustrup began developing C++ in 1979 (then called "C with Classes"), and, in his own words, "invented C++, wrote its early definitions, and produced its first implementation... chose and formulated the design criteria for C++, designed all its major facilities, and was responsible for the processing of extension proposals in the C++ standards committee." Stroustrup also wrote what many consider to be the standard text for the language, *The C++ Programming Language*, which is now in its third edition. The text has been revised twice to reflect the evolution of the language and the work of the C++ standards committee.

Education and academic work

Stroustrup has a master's degree in mathematics and computer science (1975) from the University of Aarhus, Denmark, and a Ph.D. in computer science (1979) from the University of Cambridge, England, where he was a student at Churchill College. He was the head of AT&T Lab's Large-scale Programming Research department, from its creation until late 2002. Stroustrup was elected member of the National Academy of Engineering in 2004. He is a Fellow of the ACM (1994) and an IEEE Fellow. He currently works at Texas A&M University, United States, as a Professor where he holds the College of Engineering Chair in Computer Science.

Awards

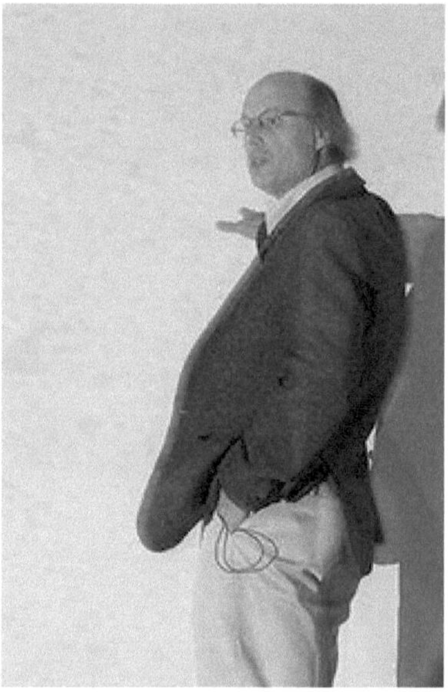

Bjarne Stroustrup giving a talk at Kent State University on C++0x in 2007.

- 1992 - ACM Grace Murray Hopper Award
- 2004 - IEEE Computer Society 2004 Computer Entrepreneur Award
- 2005 - William Procter Prize for Scientific Achievement
- 2008 - Dr. Dobb's Excellence in Programming award.

Source (edited): "http://en.wikipedia. org/wiki/Bjarne_Stroustrup"

Boost C++ Libraries

The **Boost C++ Libraries** are a collection of free libraries that extend the functionality of C++.

Overview

Most of the Boost libraries are licensed under the Boost Software License, designed to allow Boost to be used with both free and proprietary software projects. Many of Boost's founders are on the C++ standards committee and several Boost libraries have been accepted for incorporation into both the Technical Report 1 and C++0x.

The libraries are aimed at a wide range of C++ users and application domains. They range from general-purpose libraries like the smart pointer library, to operating system abstractions like *Boost FileSystem*, to libraries primarily aimed at other library developers and advanced C++ users, like the template metaprogramming (MPL) and DSL creation (Proto).

In order to ensure efficiency and flexibility, Boost makes extensive use of templates. Boost has been a source of extensive work and research into generic programming and metaprogramming in C++.

The current Boost release contains over 80 individual libraries, including libraries for linear algebra, pseudorandom number generation, multithreading, image processing, regular expressions, unit testing, and many others. The majority of Boost libraries are header based, consisting of inline functions and templates, and as such do not need to be built in advance of their usage.

Some Boost libraries coexist as independent libraries.

Associated people

Original founders of Boost still active in the community include Beman Dawes and David Abrahams. Author of several books on C++, Nicolai Josuttis contributed the Boost array library in 2001. Around 3,000 people are subscribed to Boost mail-list and dozens of them are very active (as of 2007).

List of libraries in Boost

String and text processing

- conversion/lexical_cast - lexical_cast class template, from Kevlin Henney.
- format - Type-safe 'printf-like' format operations, from Samuel Krempp.
- iostreams - Framework for defining streams, stream buffers and i/o filters, from Jonathan Turkanis.
- regex - Regular expression library, from John Maddock.
- spirit - LL parser framework represents parsers directly as Extended Backus Naur Form (EBNF) grammars in inlined C++, from Joel de Guzman, Hartmut Kaiser, Dan Nuffer and team.
- string_algo - String algorithms library, from Pavol Droba.
- tokenizer - Break of a string or other character sequence into a series of tokens, from John Bandela.
- wave - Standards conformant implementation of the mandated C99/C++ preprocessor functionality packed behind an easy to use iterator interface, from Hartmut Kaiser.
- xpressive - Regular expressions that can be written as strings or as expression templates, and that can refer to each other and themselves recursively with the power of context-free grammars, from Eric Niebler.

Containers

- array - STL compliant container wrapper for arrays of constant size, from Nicolai Josuttis.
- bimap - Bidirectional maps, from Matias Capeletto.
- circular_buffer - STL compliant container also known as ring or cyclic buffer, from Jan Gaspar.
- dynamic_bitset - A runtime sized version of std::bitset from Jeremy Siek and Chuck Allison.
- graph - Generic graph components and algorithms, from Jeremy Siek and a University of Notre Dame team.
- intrusive - Intrusive containers and algorithms, from Ion Gaztañaga.
- multi_array - Multidimensional containers and adaptors for arrays of contiguous data, from Ron Garcia.
- multi_index - Containers with multiple STL-compatible access interfaces, from Joaquín M López Muñoz.
- pointer container - Containers for storing heap-allocated polymorphic objects to ease OO-programming, from Thorsten Ottosen.
- property map - Concepts defining interfaces which map key objects to value objects, from Jeremy Siek.
- unordered - unordered associative containers, from Daniel James.
- variant - Safe, generic, stack-based discriminated union container, from Eric Friedman and Itay Maman.

Iterators

- graph - Generic graph components and algorithms, from Jeremy Siek and a University of Notre Dame team.
- iterators - Iterator construction framework, adaptors, concepts, and more, from Dave Abrahams, Jeremy Siek, and Thomas Witt.
- operators - Templates ease arithmetic classes and iterators, from Dave Abrahams and Jeremy Siek.
- tokenizer - Break of a string or other character sequence into a series of tokens, from John Bandela.

Algorithms

- foreach - BOOST_FOREACH macro for easily iterating over the elements of a sequence, from Eric Niebler.
- graph - Generic graph components and algorithms, from Jeremy Siek and a University of Notre Dame team.
- minmax - standard library extensions for simultaneous min/max and min/max element computations, from Hervé Brönnimann.
- range - A new infrastructure for generic algorithms that builds on top of the new iterator concepts, from Thorsten Ottosen. See also Range as an alternative to iterator
- string_algo - String algorithms library, from Pavol Droba.
- utility - Class next(), prior() function templates, from Dave Abrahams and others.

Function objects and higher-order programming

- bind and mem_fn - Generalized binders for function/object/pointers and member functions, from Peter Dimov.
- function - Function object wrappers for deferred calls or callbacks, from Doug Gregor.
- functional - Enhanced function

object adaptors, from Mark Rodgers.
- functional/hash - A TR1 hash function object that can be extended to hash user defined types, from Daniel James.
- lambda - Define small unnamed function objects at the actual call site, and more, from Jaakko Järvi and Gary Powell.
- ref - A utility library for passing references to generic functions, from Jaako Järvi, Peter Dimov, Doug Gregor, and Dave Abrahams.
- signals - managed signals & slots callback implementation, from Doug Gregor.
- signals2 - managed signals & slots callback implementation (thread-safe version 2), from Frank Mori Hess.
- result_of - determines the type of a function call expression.

Generic Programming

- call_traits - Defines types for passing parameters, from John Maddock, Howard Hinnant, et al.
- concept check - Tools for generic programming, from Jeremy Siek.
- enable_if - Selective inclusion of function template overloads, from Jaakko Järvi, Jeremiah Willcock, and Andrew Lumsdaine.
- function_types - Type traits for callable, built-in types, from Tobias Schwinger.
- in_place_factory, typed_in_place_factory- Generic in-place construction of contained objects with a variadic argument-list, from Fernando Cacciola.
- operators - Templates ease arithmetic classes and iterators, from Dave Abrahams and Jeremy Siek.
- property map - Concepts defining interfaces which map key objects to value objects, from Jeremy Siek.
- static_assert - Static assertions (compile time assertions), from John Maddock. (static_assert was added as a keyword to C++0x)
- type_traits - Templates for fundamental properties of types, from John Maddock, Steve Cleary, et al.

Template Metaprogramming

- function_types - Type traits for callable, built-in types, from Tobias Schwinger.
- fusion - Library for working with tuples, including various containers, algorithms, etc. From Joel de Guzman, Dan Marsden and Tobias Schwinger.
- mpl - Template metaprogramming framework of compile-time algorithms, sequences and metafunction classes, from Aleksey Gurtovoy.
- proto - Expression template library and compiler construction toolkit for domain-specific embedded languages, from Eric Niebler.
- static_assert - Static assertions (compile time assertions), from John Maddock.
- type_traits - Templates for fundamental properties of types, from John Maddock, Steve Cleary, et al.

Preprocessor Metaprogramming

- preprocessor - Preprocessor metaprogramming tools including repetition and recursion, from Vesa Karvonen and Paul Mensonides.

Concurrent Programming

- asio - Portable networking and other low-level I/O, including sockets, timers, hostname resolution, socket iostreams, serial ports, file descriptors and Windows HANDLEs, from Chris Kohlhoff.
- interprocess - Shared memory, memory mapped files, process-shared mutexes, condition variables, containers and allocators, from Ion Gaztañaga.
- MPI - Message Passing Interface library, for use in distributed-memory parallel application programming, from Douglas Gregor and Matthias Troyer.
- thread - Portable C++ multi-threading, from William Kempf.

Math and numerics

- accumulators - Framework for incremental calculation, and collection of statistical accumulators, from Eric Niebler.
- integer - Headers to ease dealing with integral types.
- interval - Extends the usual arithmetic functions to mathematical intervals, from Guillaume Melquiond, Hervé Brönnimann and Sylvain Pion.
- math - Several contributions in the domain of mathematics, from various authors.
- math/complex number algorithms - These complex number algorithms are the inverses of trigonometric functions currently present in the C++ standard, from John Maddock.
- math/common_factor - Greatest common divisor and least common multiple, from Daryle Walker.
- math/octonion - Octonions, from Hubert Holin.
- math/quaternion - Quaternions, from Hubert Holin.
- math/special_functions - A wide selection of mathematical special functions from John Maddock, Paul Bristow, Hubert Holin and Xiaogang Zhang.
- math/statistical distributions - A wide selection of univariate statistical distributions and functions that operate on them from John Maddock and Paul Bristow.
- multi_array - Multidimensional containers and adaptors for arrays of contiguous data, from Ron Garcia.
- numeric/conversion - Optimized Policy-based Numeric Conversions, from Fernando.
- operators - Templates ease arithmetic classes and iterators, from Dave Abrahams and Jeremy Siek.
- random - A complete system for random number generation, from Jens Maurer.
- rational - A rational number class, from Paul Moore.
- uBLAS - Basic linear algebra for dense, packed and sparse matrices, from Joerg Walter and Mathias Koch.

Correctness and testing

- concept check - Tools for generic programming, from Jeremy Siek.
- static_assert - Static assertions

(compile time assertions), from John Maddock.

- test - Support for simple program testing, full unit testing, and for program execution monitoring, from Gennadiy Rozental.

Data structures

- any - Safe, generic container for single values of different value types, from Kevlin Henney.
- bimap - Bidirectional maps, from Matias Capeletto.
- compressed_pair - Empty member optimization, from John Maddock, Howard Hinnant, et al.
- fusion - Library for working with tuples, including various containers, algorithms, etc. From Joel de Guzman and Dan Marsden and Tobias Schwinger.
- multi_index - Containers with multiple STL-compatible access interfaces, from Joaquín M López Muñoz.
- pointer container - Containers for storing heap-allocated polymorphic objects to ease OO-programming, from Thorsten Ottosen.
- property tree - A tree data structure especially suited to storing configuration data, from Marcin Kalicinski and Sebastian Redl.
- tuple - Ease definition of functions returning multiple values, and more, from Jaakko Järvi.
- uuid - Universally Unique Identifiers, from Andy Tompkins.
- variant - Safe, generic, stack-based discriminated union container, from Eric Friedman and Itay Maman.

Image processing

- gil - Generic Image Library, from Lubomir Bourdev and Hailin Jin.

Input/Output

- asio - Portable networking and other low-level I/O, including sockets, timers, hostname resolution, socket iostreams, serial ports, file descriptors and Windows HANDLEs, from Chris Kohlhoff.
- assign - Filling containers with constant or generated data has never been easier, from Thorsten Ottosen.
- format - Type-safe 'printf-like' format operations, from Samuel Krempp.
- io state savers - Save I/O state to prevent jumbled data, from Daryle Walker.
- iostreams - Framework for defining streams, stream buffers and i/o filters, from Jonathan Turkanis.
- program_options - Access to configuration data given on command line, in config files and other sources, from Vladimir Prus.
- serialization - Serialization of arbitrary data for persistence and marshalling, from Robert Ramey

Inter-language support

- python - Reflects C++ classes and functions into Python, from Dave Abrahams.

Memory

- pool - Memory pool management, from Steve Cleary.
- smart_ptr - Five smart pointer class templates, from Greg Colvin, Beman Dawes, Peter Dimov, and Darin Adler.
- utility - Class noncopyable plus checked_delete(), checked_array_delete(), next(), prior() function templates, plus base-from-member idiom, from Dave Abrahams and others.

Parsing

- spirit - LL parser framework represents parsers directly as EBNF grammars in inlined C++, from Joel de Guzman, Hartmut Kaiser, Dan Nuffer and team.

Programming Interfaces

- function - Function object wrappers for deferred calls or callbacks, from Doug Gregor.
- parameter - Write functions that accept arguments by name, by David Abrahams and Daniel Wallin.

Miscellaneous

- base-from-member - Idiom to initialize a base class with a member, from Daryle Walker.
- compressed_pair - Empty member optimization, from John Maddock, Howard Hinnant, et al.
- conversion - Polymorphic and lexical casts, from Dave Abrahams and Kevlin Henney.
- crc - Cyclic Redundancy Code, from Daryle Walker.
- date_time - Date-Time library from Jeff Garland.
- exception - A library for transporting of arbitrary data in exception objects, and transporting of exceptions between threads (N2179), from Emil Dotchevski.
- filesystem - Portable paths, iteration over directories, and other useful filesystem operations, from Beman Dawes.
- flyweight - Design pattern to manage large quantities of highly redundant objects, from Joaquín M López Muñoz.
- meta state machine: A very high-performance library for expressive UML2 finite state machines
- numeric/conversion - Optimized Policy-based Numeric Conversions, from Fernando Cacciola.
- optional - Discriminated-union wrapper for optional values, from Fernando Cacciola.
- polygon: Booleans/clipping, resizing/offsetting and more for planar polygons with integral coordinates.
- program_options - Access to configuration data given on command line, in config files and other sources, from Vladimir Prus.
- scope_exit - Execute arbitrary code at scope exit, from Alexander Nasonov.
- statechart - Arbitrarily complex finite state machines can be implemented in easily readable and maintainable C++ code, from Andreas Huber.
- swap - Enhanced generic swap function, from Joseph Gauterin.
- system - Operating system support, including the diagnostics support that will be part of the C++0x standard library, from Beman Dawes.
- timer - Event timer, progress timer, and progress display classes, from

Beman Dawes.

- TR1 - An implementation of the Technical Report on C++ Library Extensions, using other Boost libraries as a basis, from John Maddock.
- tribool - 3-state boolean type library, from Doug Gregor.
- typeof - Typeof operator emulation, from Arkadiy Vertleyb and Peder Holt.
- units - Zero-overhead dimensional analysis and unit/quantity manipulation and conversion, from Matthias Schabel and Steven Watanabe.
- utility - Class noncopyable plus checked_delete(), checked_array_delete(), next(), prior() function templates, plus base-from-member idiom, from Dave Abrahams and others.
- value_initialized - Wrapper for uniform-syntax value initialization, from Fernando Cacciola, based on the original idea of David Abrahams.

Source (edited): "http://en.wikipedia.org/wiki/Boost_C%2B%2B_Libraries"

C++

C++ (pronounced "see plus plus") is a statically typed, free-form, multi-paradigm, compiled, general-purpose programming language. It is regarded as an intermediate-level language, as it comprises a combination of both high-level and low-level language features. It was developed by Bjarne Stroustrup starting in 1979 at Bell Labs as an enhancement to the C language and originally named **C with Classes**. It was renamed *C++* in 1983.

C++ is one of the most popular programming languages and its application domains include systems software, application software, device drivers, embedded software, high-performance server and client applications, and entertainment software such as video games. Several groups provide both free and proprietary C++ compiler software, including the GNU Project, Microsoft, Intel and Embarcadero Technologies. C++ has greatly influenced many other popular programming languages, most notably C# and Java.

C++ is also used for hardware design, where the design is initially described in C++, then analyzed, architecturally constrained, and scheduled to create a register-transfer level hardware description language via high-level synthesis.

The language began as enhancements to C, first adding classes, then virtual functions, operator overloading, multiple inheritance, templates, and exception handling among other features. After years of development, the C++ programming language standard was ratified in 1998 as *ISO/IEC 14882:1998*. That standard is still current, but is amended by the 2003 technical corrigendum, *ISO/IEC 14882:2003*. The next standard version (known informally as C++0x, in reference to the long-standing expectation that it would be released sometime before 2010) is in development; its final draft was approved on March 25, 2011 and the formal specification is expected to be published in the summer of 2011.

History

Bjarne Stroustrup, creator of C++

Bjarne Stroustrup began work on "C with Classes" in 1979. The idea of creating a new language originated from Stroustrup's experience in programming for his Ph.D. thesis. Stroustrup found that Simula had features that were very helpful for large software development, but the language was too slow for practical use, while BCPL was fast but too low-level to be suitable for large software development. When Stroustrup started working in AT&T Bell Labs, he had the problem of analyzing the UNIX kernel with respect to distributed computing. Remembering his Ph.D. experience, Stroustrup set out to enhance the C language with Simula-like features. C was chosen because it was general-purpose, fast, portable and widely used. Besides C and Simula, some other languages that inspired him were ALGOL 68, Ada, CLU and ML. At first, the class, derived class, strong type checking, inlining, and default argument features were added to C via Stroustrup's C++ to C compiler, Cfront. The first commercial implementation of C++ was released on October 14, 1985.

In 1983, the name of the language was changed from *C with Classes* to C++ (++ being the increment operator in C). New features were added including virtual functions, function name and operator overloading, references, constants, user-controlled free-store memory control, improved type checking, and BCPL style single-line comments with two forward slashes (//). In 1985, the first edition of *The C++ Programming Language* was released, providing an important reference to the language, since there was not yet an official standard. Release 2.0 of C++ came in 1989 and the updated second edition of *The C++ Programming Language* was released in 1991. New features included multiple inheritance, abstract classes, static member functions, const member functions, and protected members. In 1990, *The Annotated C++ Reference Manual* was published. This work became the basis for the future standard. Late addition of features included templates, exceptions, namespaces, new casts, and a Boolean type.

As the C++ language evolved, the standard library evolved with it. The first addition to the C++ standard library was the stream I/O library which provided facilities to replace the traditional C functions such as printf and scanf. Later, among the most significant additions to the standard library, was large amounts of the Standard Template Library.

C++ is sometimes known as a hybrid language. It is possible to write object orientated or procedural code in the same program. This has caused some concern that some C++ programmers are still writing procedural code, but are under the impression that it is object orientated, simply because they are using C++. Often it is an amalgamation of the two. This usually causes most problems when the code is revisited or the task is taken over by another coder.

C++ continues to be used and is one of the preferred programming languages to develop professional applications.

Etymology

According to Stroustrup: "the name signifies the evolutionary nature of the changes from C". During C++'s development period, the language had been referred to as "new C", then "C with Classes". The final name is credited to Rick Mascitti (mid-1983) and was first used in December 1983. When Mascitti was questioned informally in 1992 about the naming, he indicated that it was given in a tongue-in-cheek spirit. It stems from C's "++" operator (which increments the value of a variable) and a common naming convention of using "+" to indicate an enhanced computer program. There is no language called "C plus". ABCL/c+ was the name of an earlier, unrelated programming language.

Language standard

In 1998, the C++ standards committee (the ISO/IEC JTC1/SC22/WG21 working group) standardized C++ and published the international standard *ISO/IEC 14882:1998* (informally known as *C++98*). For some years after the official release of the standard, the committee processed defect reports, and published a corrected version of the C++ standard, *ISO/IEC 14882:2003*, in 2003. In 2005, a technical report, called the "Library Technical Report 1" (often known as TR1 for short), was released. While not an official part of the standard, it specified a number of extensions to the standard library, which were expected to be included in the next version of C++. Support for TR1 is growing in almost all currently maintained C++ compilers.

The standard for the next version of the language (known informally as C++0x) is in development.

Philosophy

In *The Design and Evolution of C++* (1994), Bjarne Stroustrup describes some rules that he used for the design of C++:

- C++ is designed to be a statically typed, general-purpose language that is as efficient and portable as C
- C++ is designed to directly and comprehensively support multiple programming styles (procedural programming, data abstraction, object-oriented programming, and generic programming)
- C++ is designed to give the programmer choice, even if this makes it possible for the programmer to choose incorrectly
- C++ is designed to be as compatible with C as possible, therefore providing a smooth transition from C
- C++ avoids features that are platform specific or not general purpose
- C++ does not incur overhead for features that are not used (the "zero-overhead principle")
- C++ is designed to function without a sophisticated programming environment

Inside the C++ Object Model (Lippman, 1996) describes how compilers may convert C++ program statements into an in-memory layout. Compiler authors are, however, free to implement the standard in their own manner.

Standard library

The 1998 ANSI/ISO C++ standard consists of two parts: the core language and the C++ Standard Library; the latter includes most of the Standard Template Library (STL) and a slightly modified version of the C standard library. Many C++ libraries exist that are not part of the standard, and, using linkage specification, libraries can even be written in languages such as BASIC, C, Fortran, or Pascal. Which of these are supported is compiler-dependent.

The C++ standard library incorporates the C standard library with some small modifications to make it optimized with the C++ language. Another large part of the C++ library is based on the STL. This provides such useful tools as containers (for example vectors and lists), iterators to provide these containers with array-like access and algorithms to perform operations such as searching and sorting. Furthermore (multi)maps (associative arrays) and (multi)sets are provided, all of which export compatible interfaces. Therefore it is possible, using templates, to write generic algorithms that work with any container or on any sequence defined by iterators. As in C, the features of the library are accessed by using the #include directive to include a standard header. C++ provides 72 standard headers, of which 17 are deprecated.

The STL was originally a third-party library from HP and later SGI, before its incorporation into the C++ standard. The standard does not refer to it as "STL", as it is merely a part of the standard library, but many people still use that term to distinguish it from the rest of the library (input/output streams, internationalization, diagnostics, the C library subset, etc.).

Most C++ compilers provide an implementation of the C++ standard library, including the STL. Compiler-independent implementations of the STL, such as STLPort, also exist. Other projects also produce various custom implementations of the C++ standard library and the STL with various design goals.

Language features

C++ inherits most of C's syntax. The following is Bjarne Stroustrup's version of the Hello world program that uses the C++ standard library stream facility to write a message to standard output:

```
#include <iostream>

int main()
{
  std::cout << "Hello, world!\n";
}
```

Within functions that define a non-void return type, failure to return a value before control reaches the end of the function results in undefined behaviour (compilers typically provide the means to issue a diagnostic in such a case). The sole exception to this rule is the main function, which implicitly returns a value of zero.

Operators and operator overloading

C++ provides more than 35 operators, covering basic arithmetic, bit manipulation, indirection, comparisons, logical operations and others. Almost all operators can be overloaded for user-defined types, with a few notable exceptions such as member access (. and .*). The rich set of overloadable operators is central to using C++ as a domain-specific language. The overloadable operators are also an essential part of many advanced C++ programming techniques, such as smart pointers. Overloading an operator does not change the precedence of calculations involving the operator, nor does it change the number of operands that the operator uses (any operand may however be ignored by the operator, though it will be evaluated prior to execution). Overloaded "&&" and "||" operators lose their short-circuit evaluation property.

Templates

C++ templates enable generic programming. C++ supports both function and class templates. Templates may be parameterized by types, compile-time constants, and other templates. C++ templates are implemented by *instantiation* at compile-time. To instantiate a template, compilers substitute specific arguments for a template's parameters to generate a concrete function or class instance. Some substitutions are not possible; these are eliminated by an overload resolution policy described by the phrase "Substitution failure is not an error" (SFINAE). Templates are a powerful tool that can be used for generic programming, template metaprogramming, and code optimization, but this power implies a cost. Template use may increase code size, since each template instantiation produces a copy of the template code: one for each set of template arguments. This is in contrast to run-time generics seen in other languages (e.g. Java) where at compile-time the type is erased and a single template body is preserved.

Templates are different from macros: while both of these compile-time language features enable conditional compilation, templates are not restricted to lexical substitution. Templates are aware of the semantics and type system of their companion language, as well as all compile-time type definitions, and can perform high-level operations including programmatic flow control based on evaluation of strictly type-checked parameters. Macros are capable of conditional control over compilation based on predetermined criteria, but cannot instantiate new types, recurse, or perform type evaluation and in effect are limited to pre-compilation text-substitution and text-inclusion/exclusion. In other words, macros can control compilation flow based on pre-defined symbols but cannot, unlike templates, independently instantiate new symbols. Templates are a tool for static polymorphism (see below) and generic programming.

In addition, templates are a compile time mechanism in C++ that is Turing-complete, meaning that any computation expressible by a computer program can be computed, in some form, by a template metaprogram prior to runtime.

In summary, a template is a compile-time parameterized function or class written without knowledge of the specific arguments used to instantiate it. After instantiation, the resulting code is equivalent to code written specifically for the passed arguments. In this manner, templates provide a way to decouple generic, broadly applicable aspects of functions and classes (encoded in templates) from specific aspects (encoded in template parameters) without sacrificing performance due to abstraction.

Objects

C++ introduces object-oriented programming (OOP) features to C. It offers classes, which provide the four features commonly present in OOP (and some non-OOP) languages: abstraction, encapsulation, inheritance, and polymorphism. Objects are instances of classes created at runtime. One distinguishing feature of C++ classes compared to classes in other programming languages is support for deterministic destructors, which in turn provide support for the Resource Allocation is Initialization concept.

Encapsulation

Encapsulation is the hiding of information in order to ensure that data structures and operators are used as intended and to make the usage model more obvious to the developer. C++ provides the ability to define classes and functions as its primary encapsulation mechanisms. Within a class, members can be declared as either public, protected, or private in order to explicitly enforce encapsulation. A public member of the class is accessible to any function. A private member is accessible only to functions that are members of that class and to functions and classes explicitly granted access permission by the class ("friends"). A protected member is accessible to members of classes that inherit from the class in addition to the class itself and any friends.

The OO principle is that all of the functions (and only the functions) that access the internal representation of a type should be encapsulated within the type definition. C++ supports this (via member functions and friend functions), but does not enforce it: the programmer can declare parts or all of the representation of a type to be public, and is allowed to make public entities that are not part of the representation of the type. Therefore, C++ supports not just OO programming, but other weaker decomposition paradigms, like modular programming.

It is generally considered good practice to make all data private or protected, and to make public only those functions that are part of a minimal interface for users of the class. This hides all the details of data implementation, allowing the designer to later fundamentally change the implementation without changing the interface in any way.

Inheritance

Inheritance allows one data type to acquire properties of other data types. Inheritance from a base class may be declared as public, protected, or private. This access specifier determines whether unrelated and derived classes can access the inherited public and protected members of the base class. Only public inheritance corresponds to what is usually meant by "inheritance". The other two forms are much less frequently used. If the access specifier is omitted, a "class" inherits privately, while a "struct" inherits publicly. Base classes may be declared as virtual; this is called virtual inheritance. Virtual inheritance ensures that only one instance of a base class exists in the inheritance graph, avoiding some of the ambiguity problems of multiple inheritance.

Multiple inheritance is a C++ feature not found in most other languages, allowing a class to be derived from more than one base classes; this allows for more elaborate inheritance relationships. For example, a "Flying Cat" class can inherit from both "Cat" and "Flying Mammal". Some other languages, such as C# or Java, accomplish something similar (although more limited) by allowing inheritance of multiple interfaces while restricting the number of base classes to one (interfaces, unlike classes, provide only declarations of member functions, no implementation or member data). An interface as in C# and Java can be defined in C++ as a class containing only pure virtual functions, often known as an abstract base class or "ABC". The member functions of such an abstract base class are normally explicitly defined in the derived class, not inherited implicitly.

Polymorphism

Polymorphism enables one common interface for many implementations, and for objects to act differently under different circumstances.

C++ supports several kinds of *static* (compile-time) and *dynamic* (run-time) polymorphisms. Compile-time polymorphism does not allow for certain run-time decisions, while run-time polymorphism typically incurs a performance penalty.

Static polymorphism

Function overloading allows programs to declare multiple functions having the same name (but with different arguments). The functions are distinguished by the number or types of their formal parameters. Thus, the same function name can refer to different functions depending on the context in which it is used. The type returned by the function is not used to distinguish overloaded functions and would result in a compile-time error message.

When declaring a function, a programmer can specify for one or more parameters a default value. Doing so allows the parameters with defaults to optionally be omitted when the function is called, in which case the default arguments will be used. When a function is called with fewer arguments than there are declared parameters, explicit arguments are matched to parameters in left-to-right order, with any unmatched parameters at the end of the parameter list being assigned their default arguments. In many cases, specifying default arguments in a single function declaration is preferable to providing overloaded function definitions with different numbers of parameters.

Templates in C++ provide a sophisticated mechanism for writing generic, polymorphic code. In particular, through the Curiously Recurring Template Pattern, it's possible to implement a form of static polymorphism that closely mimics the syntax for overriding virtual functions. Since C++ templates are type-aware and Turing-complete, they can also be used to let the compiler resolve recursive conditionals and generate substantial programs through template metaprogramming. Contrary to some opinion, template code will not generate a bulk code after compilation with the proper compiler settings.

Dynamic polymorphism

Inheritance

Variable pointers (and references) to a base class type in C++ can refer to objects of any derived classes of that type in addition to objects exactly matching the variable type. This allows arrays and other kinds of containers to hold pointers to objects of differing types. Because assignment of values to variables usually occurs at run-time, this is necessarily a run-time phenomenon.

C++ also provides a dynamic_cast operator, which allows the program to safely attempt conversion of an object into an object of a more specific object type (as opposed to conversion to a more general type, which is always allowed). This feature relies on run-time type information (RTTI). Objects known to be of a certain specific type can also be cast to that type with static _cast, a purely compile-time construct that is faster and does not require RTTI.

Virtual member functions

Ordinarily, when a function in a derived class overrides a function in a base class, the function to call is determined by the type of the object. A given function is overridden when there exists no difference in the number or type of parameters between two or more definitions of that function. Hence, at compile time, it may not be possible to determine the type of the object and therefore the correct function to call, given only a base class pointer; the decision is therefore put off until runtime. This is called dynamic dispatch. Virtual member functions or *methods* allow the most specific implementation of the function to be called, according to the actual run-time type of the object. In C++ implementations, this is commonly done using virtual function tables. If the object type is known, this may be bypassed by prepending a fully qualified class name before the function call, but in general calls to virtual functions are resolved at run time.

In addition to standard member functions, operator overloads and destructors can be virtual. A general rule of thumb is that if any functions in the class are virtual, the destructor should be as well. As the type of an object at its creation is known at compile time, constructors, and by extension copy constructors, cannot be virtual. Nonetheless a situation may arise where a copy of an object needs to be created when a pointer to a derived object is passed as a pointer to a base object. In such a case, a common solution is to create a clone() (or similar) virtual function that creates and returns a copy of the derived class when called.

A member function can also be made "pure virtual" by appending it with = 0 after the closing parenthesis and before the semicolon. A class containing a pure virtual function is called an *abstract data type*. Objects cannot be created from abstract data types; they can only be derived from. Any derived class inherits the virtual function as pure and must provide a non-pure definition of it (and all other pure virtual functions) before objects of the derived class can be created. A program that attempts to create an object of a class with a pure virtual member function or inherited pure virtual member function is ill-formed.

Parsing and processing C++ source code

It is relatively difficult to write a good C++ parser with classic parsing algorithms such as LALR(1). This is partly because the C++ grammar is not LALR. Because of this, there are very few tools for analyzing or performing non-trivial transformations (e.g., refactoring) of existing code. One way to handle this difficulty is to choose a different syntax, such as Significantly Prettier and Easier C++ Syntax, which is LALR(1) parsable. More powerful parsers, such as GLR parsers, can be substantially simpler (though slower).

Parsing (in the literal sense of producing a syntax tree) is not the most difficult problem in building a C++ processing tool. Such tools must also have the same understanding of the meaning of the identifiers in the program as a compiler might have. Practical systems for processing C++ must then not only parse the source text, but be able to resolve for each identifier precisely which definition applies (e.g. they must correctly handle C++'s complex scoping rules) and what its type is, as well as the types of larger expressions.

Finally, a practical C++ processing tool must be able to handle the variety of C++ dialects used in practice (such as that supported by the GNU Compiler Collection and that of Microsoft's Visual C++) and implement appropriate analyzers, source code transformers, and regenerate source text. Combining advanced parsing algorithms such as GLR with symbol table construction and program transformation machinery can enable the construction of arbitrary C++ tools.

Compatibility

Producing a reasonably standards-compliant C++ compiler has proven to be a difficult task for compiler vendors in general. For many years, different C++ compilers implemented the C++ language to different levels of compliance to the standard, and their implementations varied widely in some areas such as partial template specialization. Recent releases of most popular C++ compilers support almost all of the C++ 1998 standard.

In order to give compiler vendors greater freedom, the C++ standards committee decided not to dictate the implementation of name mangling, exception handling, and other implementation-specific features. The downside of this decision is that object code produced by different compilers is expected to be incompatible. There were, however, attempts to standardize compilers for particular machines or operating systems (for example C++ ABI), though they seem to be largely abandoned now.

Exported templates

One particular point of contention is the export keyword, intended to allow template definitions to be separated from their declarations. The first widely available compiler to implement export was Comeau C/C++, in early 2003 (five years after the release of the standard); in 2004, the beta compiler of Borland C ++ Builder X was also released with export. Both of these compilers are based on the EDG C++ front end. Other compilers such as GCC do not support it at all. *Beginning ANSI C++* by Ivor Horton provides example code with the keyword that will not compile in most compilers, without reference to this problem. Herb Sutter, former convener of the C++ standards committee, recommended that export be removed from future versions of the C++ standard. During the March 2010 ISO C++ standards meeting, the C++ standards committee voted to remove exported templates entirely from C++0x, but reserve the keyword for future use.

With C

C++ is often considered to be a superset of C, but this is not strictly true. Most C code can easily be made to compile correctly in C++, but there are a few differences that cause some valid C code to be invalid or behave differently in C++.

One commonly encountered difference is that C allows implicit conversion from void* to other pointer types, but C++ does not. Another common portability issue is that C++ defines many new keywords, such as new and class, that may be used as identifiers (e.g. variable names) in a C program.

Some incompatibilities have been removed by the latest (C99) C standard, which now supports C++ features such as line comments (//), and mixed declarations and code. On the other hand, C99 introduced a number of new features that C++ does not support, such as variable-length arrays, native complex-number types, designated initializers, and compound literals. However, at least some of the new C99 features will likely be included in the next version of the C++ standard, C++0x:

- C99 preprocessor (including variadic macros, wide/narrow literal concatenation, wider integer arithmetic)
- _Pragma()
- long long
- __func__
- Headers:
  - cstdbool (stdbool.h)
  - cstdint (stdint.h)
  - cinttypes (inttypes.h).

In order to intermix C and C++ code, any function declaration or definition that is to be called from/used both in C and C++ must be declared with C linkage by placing it within an extern "C" {/*...*/} block. Such a function may not rely on features depending on name mangling (i.e., function overloading).

Criticism

Due to its large feature set and oft-perceived "strict" syntax, the language is sometimes criticized as being overly complicated and thus difficult to fully master. Because it includes most of the C programming language as a subset, C++ also inherits many of the criticisms leveled at C.

Other criticisms stem from what is missing from C++, such as a lack of "native" multithreading facilities—a feature present in some other languages, including Ada, C#, and Java (see Lock). The upcoming C++0x standard addresses this issue by adding direct support for concurrency to the language, but at present this is only possible by using operating system calls or third party libraries.

C++ is also sometimes compared unfavorably with languages such as Eiffel, Java, or Smalltalk on the basis that it enables programmers to "mix and match" declarative, functional, generic, modular, and procedural programming styles with object-oriented programming, rather than strictly enforcing a single style, although C++ is intentionally a multi-paradigm language.

A fictitious article was written, wherein Bjarne Stroustrup is supposedly interviewed for a 1998 issue of IEEE's 'Computer' magazine. In this article, the interviewer expects to discuss the successes of C++ now that several years had passed after its introduction. Instead, the impostor posing as Stroustrup proceeds to "confess" that his invention of C++ was intended to create the most complex and difficult language possible to weed out amateur programmers and raise the salaries of the few programmers who could master the language. The article contains various criticisms of C++'s complexity and poor usability, most false or exaggerated. In reality, Stroustrup wrote no such article, and due to the pervasiveness of the hoax, was compelled to publish an official denial on his website.

Richard Stallman criticizes C++ for having ambiguous grammar and "gratuitous, trivial, incompatibilities with C (...) that are of no *great* benefit".

Linus Torvalds has said, "C++ is a horrible language. It's made more horrible by the fact that a lot of substandard programmers use it".

C++ is commonly criticized for lacking built-in garbage collection. On his website, Stroustrup explains that automated memory management is routinely implemented directly in C++, without need for a built-in collector, using "smart pointer" classes. Garbage collection not based on reference counting is possible in C++ through external libraries.

The major cause of complaints is C++['s] undoubted success. As someone remarked: There are only two kinds of programming languages: those people always bitch about and those nobody uses.

—Bjarne Stroustrup, comp.lang.c++

Another point of criticism is the feature of multiple inheritance, as such ontologies are difficult to maintain.

Source (edited): "http://en.wikipedia.org/wiki/C%2B%2B"

C++0x

C++0x (pronounced "see plus plus oh ex") is the unofficial name of the planned new standard for the C++ programming language (originally, finalization was expected in 2008 or 2009, but the "0x" was retained). C++0x is intended to replace the existing C++ standard, ISO/IEC 14882, which was published in 1998 and updated in 2003. These predecessors are informally but commonly known as C++98 and C++03. The new standard will include several additions to the core language and will extend the C++ standard library, incorporating most of the C++ Technical Report 1 (TR1) libraries — most likely with the exception of the library of mathematical special functions. Since the standard is not yet finalized, this article may not reflect the most recent state of C++0x. The first working draft international standard was published in August 2010 (N3126), with the last *working* draft being (N3291) dated 5 April 2011.

In their March 2011 meeting, the ISO/IEC JTC1/SC22/WG21 C++ Standards Committee voted C++0x (N3290) to Final Draft International Standard (FDIS) status. This means that this *final* draft, dated 11 April 2011, is ready for review and approval by the ISO; the final specification is expected to be published sometime in mid-2011. To be able to finish closer to schedule, the Committee decided to focus its efforts on the solutions introduced up until 2006 and ignore newer proposals.

Candidate changes for the impending standard update

The modifications for C++ will involve both the core language and the standard library.

In the development of every utility of the new standard, the committee has applied some directives:

- Maintain stability and compatibility with C++98 and possibly with C;
- Prefer introduction of new features through the standard library, rather than extending the core language;
- Prefer changes that can evolve programming technique;

- Improve C++ to facilitate systems and library design, rather than to introduce new features only useful to specific applications;
- Increase type safety by providing safer alternatives to current, unsafe techniques;
- Increase performance and the ability to work directly with hardware;
- Provide proper solutions for real world problems;
- Implement "zero-overhead" principle (additional support required by some utilities must be used only if the utility is used);
- Make C++ easy to teach and to learn without removing any utility needed by expert programmers.

Attention to beginners is considered important, because they will always compose the majority of computer programmers, and because many beginners would not intend to extend their knowledge of C++, limiting themselves to operate in the aspects of the language in which they are specialized. Additionally, considering the vastness of C++ and its usage (including areas of application and programming styles), even the most experienced programmers can become beginners in a new programming paradigm.

Extensions to the C++ core language

One function of the C++ committee is the development of the language core. The presentation date of C++0x depends on the progress of this part of the standard.

Areas of the core language that will be significantly improved include multithreading support, generic programming support, uniform initialization, and performance enhancements.

For the purposes of this article, core language features and changes are grouped into 4 general sections: run-time performance enhancements, build-time performance enhancements, usability enhancements, or new functionality. Some features could fall into multiple groups, but they will only be mentioned in the group which primarily represents that feature.

Core language runtime performance enhancements

These language features primarily exist to provide some kind of performance benefit, either of memory or of computational speed.

Source (edited): "http://en.wikipedia.org/wiki/C%2B%2B0x"

C++ Report

C++ Report was a bi-monthly professional computer magazine published by SIGS Publications Group. It has been edited by Douglas C. Schmidt, Brad Appleton and Robert Cecil Martin and aimed to cover various issues related to C++ programming language. It has been widely recognized as one of very important publications related to C++,. In particular, in 1995 it has published an article *Exception Handling: A False Sense of Security* by Tom Cargill.

Notable Contributors

- Douglas C. Schmidt
- Robert Cecil Martin
- Scott Meyers
- Tom Cargill
- Jim Coplien (a.k.a. James O. Coplien)
- David Abrahams
- Andrew Koenig

Source (edited): "http://en.wikipedia.org/wiki/C%2B%2B_Report"

C++ classes

The C++ programming language allows programmers to separate program-specific datatypes through the use of **classes**. Instances of these datatypes are known as objects and can contain member variables, constants, member functions, and overloaded operators defined by the programmer. Syntactically, classes are extensions of the C struct, which cannot contain functions or overloaded operators.

Differences between struct and classes in C++

In C++, a *structure* is a class defined with the struct keyword. Its members and base classes are public by default. A class defined with the class keyword has private members and base classes by default. This is the only difference between structs and classes in C++.

Aggregate classes

An aggregate class is a class with no user-declared constructors, no private or protected non-static data members, no base classes, and no virtual functions. Such a class can be initialized with a brace-enclosed comma-separated list of initializer-clauses. The following code has the same semantics in both C and C++:

```
struct C
{
 int a;
 double b;
};

struct D
{
 int a;
 double b;
 C c;
};

// initialize an object of type C with an
initializer-list
C c = {1, 2};

// D has a sub-aggregate of type C. In
such cases initializer-clauses can be
nested
D d = {10, 20, {1, 2}};
```

POD-structs

A POD-struct (Plain Old Data Structure) is an aggregate class that has no non-static data members of type non-POD-struct, non-POD-union (or array of such types) or reference, and has no user-defined assignment operator and no user-defined destructor. A POD-struct could be said to be the C++ equivalent of a C struct. In most cases, a POD-struct will have the same memory layout as a corresponding struct declared in C. For this reason, POD-structs are sometimes colloquially referred to as "C-style structs".

Properties shared between structs in C and POD-structs in C++

- Data members are allocated so that later members have higher addresses within an object, except where separated by an access-specifier.
- Two POD-struct types are layout-compatible if they have the same number of nonstatic data members, and corresponding nonstatic data members (in order) have layout-compatible types.
- A POD-struct may contain unnamed padding.
- A pointer to a POD-struct object, suitably converted using a reinterpret cast, points to its initial member and vice versa, implying that there is no padding at the beginning of a POD-struct.
- A POD-struct may be used with the offsetof macro.

Declaration and usage

C++ classes have their own members. These members include variables (including other structures and classes), functions (specific identifiers or overloaded operators) known as methods, constructors and destructors. Members are declared to be either publicly or privately accessible using the public: and private: access specifiers respectively. Any member encountered after a specifier will have the associated access until another specifier is encountered. There is also inheritance between classes which can make use of the protected: specifier.

Basic declaration and member variables

Classes are declared with the class or struct keyword. Declaration of members are placed within this declaration.

The above definitions are functionally equivalent. Either code will define objects of type person as having two public data members, name and age. The semicolons after the closing braces are mandatory.

After one of these declarations (but not both), person can be used as follows to create newly defined variables of the person datatype:

```
#include <iostream>
#include <string>
using namespace std;

class person
{
public:
 string name;
 int age;
};

int main()
{
 person a, b;
 a.name = "Calvin";
 b.name = "Hobbes";
 a.age = 30;
 b.age = 20;
 cout << a.name << ": " << a.age <<
endl;
 cout << b.name << ": " << b.age <<
endl;
 return 0;
}
```

Executing the above code will output

```
Calvin: 30
Hobbes: 20
```

Member functions

An important feature of the C++ class and structure are **member functions**. Each datatype can have its own built-in functions (referred to as methods) that have access to all (public and private) members of the datatype. In the body of these non-static member functions, the keyword this can be used to refer to the object for which the function is called. This is commonly implemented by passing the address of the object as an implicit first argument to the function. Take the above person type as an example again:

```
class person
{
  std::string name;
  int age;
public:
  person() : age(5) { }
  void print() const;
};

void person::print() const
{
  cout << name << ";" << age << endl;
  /* "name" and "age" are the member variables.
     The "this" keyword is an expression whose value is the address
     of the object for which the member was invoked. Its type is
     const person*, because the function is declared const.
  */
}
```

In the above example the print() function is declared in the body of the class and defined by qualifying it with the name of the class followed by ::. Both name and age are private (default for class) and print() is declared as public which is necessary if it is to be used from outside the class.

With the member function print(), printing can be simplified into:

```
a.print();
b.print();
```

where a and b above are called senders, and each of them will refer to their own member variables when the print() function is executed.

It is common practice to separate the class or structure declaration (called its interface) and the definition (called its implementation) into separate units. The interface, needed by the user, is kept in a header and the implementation is kept separately in either source or compiled form.

Inheritance

The layout of non-POD classes in memory is not specified by the C++ standard. For example, many popular C++ compilers implement single inheritance by concatenation of the parent class fields with the child class fields, but this is not required by the standard. This choice of layout makes referring to a derived class via a pointer to the parent class type a trivial operation.

For example, consider

```
class P
{
  int x;
};


class C : public P
{
  int y;
};
```

An instance of P with a P* p pointing to it might look like this in memory:

```
+----+
|P::x|
+----+
↑
p
```

An instance of C with a P* p pointing to it might look like this:

```
+----+----+
|P::x|C::y|
+----+----+
↑
p
```

Therefore, any code that manipulates the fields of a P object can manipulate the P fields inside the C object without having to consider anything about the definition of C's fields. A properly-written C++ program shouldn't make any assumptions about the layout of inherited fields, in any case. Using the static_cast or dynamic_cast type conversion operators will ensure that pointers are properly converted from one type to another.

Multiple inheritance is not as simple. If a class D inherits P1 and P2, then the fields of both parents need to be stored in some order, but (at most) only one of the parent classes can be located at the front of the derived class. Whenever the compiler needs to convert a pointer from the D type to either P1 or P2, the compiler will provide an automatic conversion from the address of the derived class to the address of the base class fields (typically, this is a simple offset calculation).

For more on multiple inheritance, see virtual inheritance.

Overloaded operators

In C++, operators, such as + - * /, can be overloaded to suit the needs of programmers. These operators are called **overloadable operators**.

By convention, overloaded operators should behave nearly the same as they do in built-in datatypes (int, float, etc.), but this is not required. One can declare a structure called integer in which the variable *really* stores an integer, but by calling integer * integer the sum, instead of the product, of the integers might be returned:

```
struct integer
{
  int i;
  integer(int j = 0) : i(j) {}
  integer operator*(const integer &k) const
  {
    return integer (i + k.i);
  }
};
```

The code above made use of a constructor to "construct" the return value. For clearer presentation (although this could decrease efficiency of the program if the compiler cannot optimize the statement into the equivalent one above), the above code can be rewritten as:

```
integer operator*(const integer &k) const
{
  integer m;
  m.i = i + k.i;
  return m;
}
```

Programmers can also put a prototype of the operator in the struct declaration and define the function of the operator in the global scope:

```
struct integer
{
   int i;

   integer(int j = 0) : i(j) {}

   integer operator*(const integer &k)
const;
};

integer integer::operator*(const integer
&k) const
{
   return integer(i + k.i);
}
```

i above represents the sender's own member variable, while k.i represents the member variable from the argument variable k.

The const keyword appears twice in the above code. The first occurrence, the argument const integer &k, indicated that the argument variable will not be changed by the function. The second incidence at the end of the declaration promises the compiler that the sender would not be changed by the function run.

In const integer &k, the ampersand (&) means "pass by reference". When the function is called, a pointer to the variable will be passed to the function, rather than the value of the variable.

The same overloading properties above apply also to classes.

Note that arity, associativity and precedence of operators cannot be changed.

Binary overloadable operators

Binary operators (operators with two arguments) are overloaded by declaring a function with an "identifier" *operator (something)* which calls one single argument. The variable on the left of the operator is the sender while that on the right is the argument.

```
integer i = 1;
/* we can initialize a structure variable
this way as
  if calling a constructor with only the
first
  argument specified. */
integer j = 3;
/* variable names are independent of
the names of the
  member variables of the structure. */
integer k = i * j;
cout << k.i << endl;
```

'4' would be printed.

The following is a list of binary overloadable operators:

The '=' (assignment) operator between two variables of the same structure type is overloaded by default to copy the entire content of the variables from one to another. It can be overwritten with something else, if necessary.

Operators must be overloaded one by one, in other words, no overloading is associated with one another. For example, < is not necessarily the opposite of >.

Unary overloadable operators

While some operators, as specified above, takes two terms, sender on the left and the argument on the right, some operators have only one argument - the sender, and they are said to be "unary". Examples are the negative sign (when nothing is put on the left of it) and the "logical NOT" (exclamation mark, !).

Sender of unary operators may be on the left or on the right of the operator. The following is a list of unary overloadable operators:

The syntax of an overloading of a unary operator, where the sender is on the right, is as follows:

return_type operator@ ()

When the sender is on the left, the declaration is:

return_type operator@ (int)

@ above stands for the operator to be overloaded. Replace return_type with the datatype of the return value (int, bool, structures etc.)

The int parameter essentially means nothing but a convention to show that the sender is on the left of the operator.

const arguments can be added to the end of the declaration if applicable.

The square bracket [] and the round bracket () can be overloaded in C++ structures. The square bracket must contain exactly one argument, while the round bracket can contain any specific number of arguments, or no arguments.

The following declaration overloads the square bracket.

return_type operator[] (*argument*)

The content inside the bracket is specified in the argument part.

Round bracket is overloaded a similar way.

return_type operator() (*arg1, arg2, ...*)

Contents of the bracket in the operator call are specified in the second bracket.

In addition to the operators specified above, the arrow operator (->), the starred arrow (->*), the new keyword and the delete keyword can also be overloaded. These memory-or-pointer-related operators must process memory-allocating functions after overloading. Like the assignment (=) operator, they are also overloaded by default if no specific declaration is made.

Sometimes software engineers may want their variables to take a default or specific value upon declaration. This can be done by declaring constructors.

```
person(string N, int A)
{
  name = N;
  age = A;
}
```

Member variables can be initialized in an initializer list, with utilization of a colon, as in the example below. This differs from the above in that it initializes (using the constructor), rather than using the assignment operator. This is more efficient for class types, since it just needs to be constructed directly; whereas with assignment, they must be first initialized using the default constructor, and then assigned a different value. Also some types (like references and const types) cannot be assigned to and therefore must be initialized in the initializer list.

```
person(std::string N, int A) : name(N),
age(A) {}
```

Note that the curly braces cannot be omitted, even if empty.

Default values can be given to the last arguments to help initializing default values.

```
person(std::string N = "", int A = 0) :
name(N), age(A) {}
```

When no arguments are given to the constructor in the example above, it is equivalent to calling the following constructor with no arguments (a default constructor):

```
person() : name(""), age(0) {}
```

The declaration of a constructor looks like a function with the name as the same as the datatype. In fact, we can really call the constructor in form of a function call. In that case a person type variable would be the return value:

```
int main()
{
  person r = person("Wales", 40);
  r.print();
}
```

The above code creates a temporary person object, and then assigns it to r using the copy constructor. A better way of creating the object (without unnecessary copying) is:

```
int main()
{
  person r ("Wales", 40);
  r.print ();
}
```

Specific program actions, which may or may not relate to the variable, can be added as part of the constructor.

```
person()
{
  std::cout << "Hello!" << endl;
}
```

With the above constructor, a "Hello!" will be printed in case a person variable with no specific value is initialized.

A destructor is the reverse of a constructor. It is called when an instance of a class is destroyed, e.g. when an object of a class created in a block (set of curly braces "{}") is deleted after the closing brace, then the destructor is called automatically. It will be called upon emptying of the memory location storing the variable. Destructors can be used to release resources, such as heap-allocated memory and opened files when an instance of that class is destroyed.

The syntax for declaring a destructor is similar to that of a constructor. There is no return value and the name of the method is the same as the name of the class with a tilde (~) in front.

```
~person()
{
  cout << "I'm deleting " << name <<
" with age " << age << endl;
}
```

Class templates

In C++, class declarations can be generated from class templates. Such class templates represent a family of classes. An actual class declaration is obtained by *instantiating* the template with one or more template arguments. A template instantiated with a particular set of arguments is called a template specialization.

Properties

The syntax of C++ tries to make every aspect of a structure look like that of the basic datatypes. Therefore, overloaded operators allow structures to be manipulated just like integers and floating-point numbers, arrays of structures can be declared with the square-bracket syntax (some_structure variable _name[size]), and pointers to structures can be dereferenced in the same way as pointers to built-in datatypes.

Memory consumption

The memory consumption of a structure is at least the sum of the memory sizes of constituent variables. Take the twonums structure below as an example.

```
struct twonums
{
  int a;
  int b;
};
```

The structure consists of two integers. In many current C++ compilers, integers are 32-bit integers by default, so each of the member variables consume four bytes of memory. The entire structure, therefore, consumes at least (or exactly) eight bytes of memory, as follows.

```
+----+----+
| a  | b  |
+----+----+
```

However, the compiler may add padding between the variables or at the end of the structure to ensure proper data alignment for a given computer architecture, often padding variables to be 32-bit aligned. For example, the structure

```
struct bytes_and_such
{
  char c;
  char C;
  short int s;
  int i;
  double d;
};
```

could look like

```
+-+-+--+--+--+--+--------+
|c|C|XX|s | i |  d     |
+-+-+--+--+--+--+--------+
```

in memory, where XX is two unused bytes.

As structures may make use of pointers and arrays to declare and initialize its member variables, memory consumption of structures is not necessarily constant. Another example of non-constant memory size is template structures.

Source (edited): "http://en.wikipedia.org/wiki/C%2B%2B_classes"

CFLAGS

CFLAGS and **CXXFLAGS** are either the name of environment variables or of Makefile variables that can be set to specify additional switches to be passed to a compiler in the process of building computer software.

These variables are usually set inside a Makefile and are then appended to the command line when the compiler is invoked. If they are not specified in the Makefile, then they will be read from the environment, if present. Tools like autoconf's ./configure script will usually pick them up from the environment and write them into the generated Makefiles.

CFLAGS allows to add switches for the C compiler, while **CXXFLAGS** is meant to be used when invoking a C ++ compiler. Similarly, a variable **CPPFLAGS** exists with switches to be passed to the C preprocessor.

These variables are most commonly used to specify optimization or debugging switches to a compiler, as for example -g, -O2 or (GCC-specific) -march =athlon.

Source (edited): "http://en.wikipedia.org/wiki/CFLAGS"

Carbide.c++

Carbide.c++ is a software development tool for C++ development on Symbian OS. It is used to develop phones that use the OS, as well as applications that run on those phones. It is based on the Eclipse IDE platform enhanced with extra plug-ins to support Symbian OS development. The product is provided by the Symbian Foundation under an open source model. In April 2009, Nokia transferred Carbide.c++ and many other software developer tools to the Symbian Foundation. Members of the Symbian community now manage and contribute code to the Carbide.c++ product.

Tool Packages

Carbide.c++ is provided by the Symbian Foundation in two different tool packages.

- Application Development Toolkit (ADT) contains tools for application development, including the IDE, debugger, and analysis tools.
- Product Development Toolkit (PDT) contains tools for contribution and product creation.

Both the ADT and PDT are basic installers that include Carbide.c++, several Eclipse-based plug-ins and several stand-alone tools.

ADT/PDT v1 contains Carbide.c++ v2.0.4

ADT/PDT v2 (Q4 2009) is targeted to contain Carbide.c++ v2.2

Technology

Carbide.c++ is based on the latest versions of Eclipse IDE and Eclipse CDT extended with Symbian OS -specific features. Currently it supports the WINSCW x86 C++ compiler found in CodeWarrior for production of emulator binaries. For target binaries it supports GCC, and ARM RVCT compilers (sold separately). The WINSCW and GCC compilers are actually provided in the SDK and not explicitly included in the Carbide IDE.

Carbide.c++ has branched very few parts of CDT - nearly all of it is contained within added plug-ins added on top of Eclipse. The few branches mostly relate to the different semantics of the CodeWarrior debugger engine, compared to GDB which is what Eclipse previously supported. Because Carbide.c++ is very similar to a standard Eclipse installation, it can still be used for other types of development such as Java or Perl (provided the correct plug-ins are installed using Eclipse's self-update mechanism). Similarly, it ought to be possible to produce a product with similar functionality to Carbide.c++ by moving the Carbide.c++ plug-ins into a standard Eclipse installation; this is not currently a facility offered by Nokia.

Carbide.c++ supports the Symbian Build System v1 and v2 (aka Raptor). The former is a perl-based build system and the latter is built using Python and supports the next generation Symbian OS operating systems. The main advantage of supporting SBSv1 and v2 in Carbide is users can create command-line builds in parallel with IDE builds and not have to manage two different workspaces. The disadvantage of SBSv1 is dependency checking is automatic on every build and re-building large projects to take a while. Carbide.c++ built in some short cuts (starting with v1.3) to speed up rebuilds.

Early versions of Carbide (v1.0, 1.1) supported a different build method which had many problems.

History

Carbide.c++ development tools family was created to replace CodeWarrior for Symbian OS as the primary development environment for Symbian OS. Adoption of the tool has been slow but CodeWarrior usage is diminishing since the older tool no longer supports the latest changes to Symbian OS and S60 platforms.

Carbide was provided as three commercial products and one free product. Today the product is part of the Symbian Foundation offering and is completely free.

- Express—Basic tools for application development. Contains project management, code authoring, emulator & GCC-E builds, and emulator debugging. The Express edition was provided for free and did not support development directly on production phones.
- Developer Edition—Targeted at aftermarket software development. Contained Express features, a UI Designer (for rapid UI creation), and application-level on-device debugging for S60 and UIQ phones.

- Professional—Targeted at Symbian OS phone manufacturers, their partners, and application/ middleware vendors working on demanding projects. Contained Developer features, system-level on-device debugging, and performance profiling tools.
- OEM—Targeted at early-access embedded development such as driver-development, base porting, and hardware-dependent application and middleware development. Contained Professional features, and stop-mode debugging using Lauterbach and Sophia in-circuit emulators.

The products ranged in price from 300 to 8000 Euros depending on features set and licensing model.

Carbide had a slow reception to the Symbian community. Developers are generally not fond of moving to new tools and early versions of Carbide had problems. There were several frequently cited complaints - for example, lack of Symbian-OS-style code indenting, lack of an easy "find in files" facility, speed of import of Symbian OS build files (MMPs), and difficulties using on-device debugging. In addition, the much-anticipated Managed Build System did not work properly - rather than offering a true incremental build, it frequently deleted everything and started again. Otherwise the reception was warm - the development environment is preferred to CodeWarrior, the IDE is based on Java so there are some speed and memory concerns, the IDE is often slow and has a pretty big memory foot print, all trademarks of the Java environment.

Carbide.c++ has made steady progress in addressing issues brought up by the developer community. CodeWarrior usage has dropped off significantly due to improvements in Carbide and CodeWarrior's lack of support for the newer versions of Symbian OS.

Using Carbide.c++

To do Symbian OS C++ development you need the Carbide.c++ IDE and a Symbian OS-based SDK. This SDK contains the emulator and also the libraries and header files required for Symbian OS development. Development kits are available at Forum Nokia and the Symbian Foundation web sites. Please note that these kits may have different names reflecting additional capabilities (Cust kits, Developer Kits, PDK, iSSK).

Source (edited): "http://en.wikipedia.org/wiki/Carbide.c%2B%2B"

Circular dependency

In software engineering, a **circular dependency** is a relation between two or more modules which either directly or indirectly depend on each other to function properly.

Overview

Circular dependencies are natural in many domain models where certain objects of the same domain depend on each other. However, in software design circular dependencies between larger software modules are considered an anti-pattern because of their negative effects.

Problems of circular dependencies

Circular dependencies can cause many unwanted effects in software programs. Most problematic from a software design point of view is the *tight coupling* of the mutually dependent modules which reduces or makes impossible the separate re-use of a single module.

Circular dependencies can cause a domino effect when a small local change in one module spreads into other modules and has unwanted global effects (program errors, compile errors). Circular dependencies can also result in infinite recursions or other unexpected failures.

Circular dependencies may also cause memory leaks by preventing certain very primitive automatic garbage collectors (those that use reference counting) from deallocating unused objects.

Causes and solutions

In very large software designs, software engineers may lose the context and inadvertently introduce circular dependencies. There are tools to analyze software and find unwanted circular dependencies.

Circular dependencies are often introduced by inexperienced programmers who need to implement some kind of callback functionality. Experienced programmers avoid such unnecessary circular dependencies by applying design patterns like the observer pattern.

Example of circular dependencies in C++

Implementation of circular dependencies in C/C++ can be a bit tricky, because any class or structure definition must be placed above its usage in the same file. A circular dependency between classes *A* and *B* will thus both require the definition of *A* to be placed above *B*, and the definition of *B* to be placed above *A*, which of course is impossible. A forward declaration trick is therefore needed to accomplish this.

The following example illustrates how this is done.

- File **a.h**:

```
#ifndef A_H
#define A_H

class B;      //forward declaration

class A {
public:
      B* b;
};
#endif //A_H
```

- File **b.h**:

```
#ifndef B_H
#define B_H

class A;      //forward declaration

class B {
public:
      A* a;
};
#endif //B_H
```

- File **main.cpp**:

```
#include "a.h"
#include "b.h"

int main() {
      A a;
      B b;
      a.b = &b;
      b.a = &a;
}
```

Note that although a name (e.g. A) can be *declared* multiple times, such as in forward declarations, it can only be *defined* once (the One Definition Rule).

Source (edited): "http://en.wikipedia.org/wiki/Circular_dependency"

CodeSynthesis XSD

CodeSynthesis XSD is an XML Data Binding compiler for C++ developed by Code Synthesis and dual-licensed under the GNU GPL and a proprietary license. Given an XML instance specification (XML Schema), it generates C++ classes that represent the given vocabulary as well as parsing and serialization code. It is supported on a large number of platforms, including AIX, GNU/Linux, HP-UX, Mac OS X, Solaris, Windows, HP OpenVMS, and IBM z/OS. Supported C++ compilers include GNU G++, Intel C++, HP aCC, Sun C++, IBM XL C ++, and Microsoft Visual C++. A version for mobile and embedded systems, called CodeSynthesis XSD/e, is also available.

One of the unique features of CodeSynthesis XSD is its support for two different XML Schema to C++ mappings: in-memory C++/Tree and stream-oriented C++/Parser. The C++/Tree mapping is a traditional mapping with a tree-like, in-memory data structure. C++/Parser is a new, SAX-like mapping which represents the information stored in XML instance documents as a hierarchy of vocabulary-specific parsing events. In comparison to C++/Tree, the C++/Parser mapping allows one to handle large XML documents that would not fit in memory, perform stream-oriented processing, or use an existing in-memory representation.

CodeSynthesis XSD itself is written in C++.

Source (edited): "http://en.wikipedia.org/wiki/CodeSynthesis_XSD"

Comparison of Java and C++

This is a **comparison of the Java programming language with the C++ programming language**.

Design aims

The differences between the C++ and Java programming languages can be traced to their heritage, as they have different design goals.

- **C++** was designed mainly for systems programming, extending the C programming language. To this procedural programming language designed for efficient execution, C++ has added support for statically-typed object-oriented programming, exception handling, scoped resource management, and generic programming, in particular. It also added a standard library which includes generic containers and algorithms.
- **Java** was created initially to support network computing. It relies on a virtual machine to be secure and highly portable. It is bundled with an extensive library designed to provide a complete abstraction of the underlying platform. Java is a statically-typed object-oriented language that uses a syntax similar to C++, but is not compatible with it. It was designed from scratch, with the goal of being easy to use and accessible to a wider audience.

The different goals in the development of C++ and Java resulted in different principles and design trade-offs between the languages. The differences are as follows :

C++ is a powerful language designed for system programming. The Java language was designed to be simple and easy to learn with a powerful cross-platform library. The Java standard library is considerably large for a standard library. However, Java does not always provide full access to the features and performance of the platform on which the software runs. The C++ standard libraries are simple and robust providing containers and associative arrays.

Language features

Syntax

- Java syntax has a context free grammar which can be parsed by a simple LALR parser. Parsing C++ is somewhat more complicated; for example, Foo<1>(3); is a sequence of comparisons if Foo is a variable, but it creates an object if Foo is the name of a class template.
- C++ allows namespace level constants, variables, and functions. All such Java declarations must be inside a class or interface.
- In C++ declarations, a class name declares an object of that class as a value (a.k.a. value semantics). There

is no way to do this in Java. Objects are not values in Java. In Java declarations, a class name declares a *reference* to an object of that class (a.k.a. reference semantics). The equivalent way to do this in C++ is to use "*" to declare a pointer.

- In C++, the operator "." takes an object as the left operand and accesses a member of the object. Since objects cannot be values in Java, and all objects are accessed through references, this cannot be done in Java. In Java, the "." operator takes a *reference* to an object as the left operand and access a member of that object. The equivalent operator in C++ is "->".
- In C++, it is possible to declare a pointer to a const type, that is, you cannot modify the object pointed to by the pointer using that pointer. Functions and methods can also guarantee that they will not modify the object pointed to by a pointer by using the "const" keyword. This enforces const-correctness. This is not possible in Java. You can declare a reference "final" in Java (like declaring a pointer "const" in C++), but this just prevents you from re-binding that reference; you can still modify the object referenced by the reference.
- C++ supports goto statements; Java enforces structured control flow, and relies on labelled break and labelled continue statements to provide some goto-like functionality. Some commenters point out that these labelled flow control statements break the single point-of-exit property of structured programming.
- C++ provides low-level features which Java lacks. In C++, pointers can be used to manipulate specific memory locations, a task necessary for writing low-level operating system components. Similarly, many C++ compilers support inline assembler. In Java, such code has to reside in external libraries, and can only be accessed through the Java Native Interface with a significant overhead for each call.

Semantics

- C++ allows default values for arguments of a function/method, Java does not. However, method overloading can be used to obtain similar results in Java.
- The minimal compilation unit in C++ is a function; the compilation unit in Java is a class. In C++, functions can be compiled separately. In Java, to compile and maintain methods separately requires moving them into super and extended classes or using some other code refactoring technique.
- C++ allows a range of implicit conversions between native types, and also allows the programmer to define implicit conversions involving user-defined types. In Java, only widening conversions between native types are implicit; other conversions require explicit cast syntax.
  - A consequence of this is that although loop conditions (if, while and the exit condition in for) in Java and C++ both expect a boolean expression, code such as if(a = 5) will cause a compile error in Java because there is no implicit narrowing conversion from int to boolean. This is handy if the code was a typo for if(a = = 5). Yet current C++ compilers usually generate a warning when such an assignment is performed within a conditional expression.
- For passing parameters to functions, C++ supports both pass-by-reference and pass-by-value. In Java, primitive parameters are always passed by value. Class types, interface types, and array types are collectively called reference types in Java and object references are passed by value.
- Java built-in types are of a specified size and range defined by the virtual machine; In C++, a minimal range of values is defined for built-in types, but the exact representation (number of bits) can be mapped to whatever native types are supported on a given platform.
  - For instance, Java characters are 16-bit Unicode characters, and strings are composed of a sequence of such characters. C++ offers both narrow and wide characters, but the actual size of each is platform dependent, as is the character set used. Strings can be formed from either type.
- The rounding and precision of floating point values and operations in C++ is platform dependent. Java provides an optional strict floating-point model that guarantees consistent results across platforms, though possibly at the cost of slower run-time performance.
- In C++, pointers can be manipulated directly as memory address values. Java references are pointers but these references can refer only to objects and arrays. Java references do not allow direct access to memory addresses or allow memory addresses to be manipulated with pointer arithmetic. In C++ one can construct pointers to pointers, pointers to ints and doubles, and pointers to arbitrary memory locations. Java references only access objects and arrays, never primitives, other references, or arbitrary memory locations.
- In C++, pointers can point to functions or methods (function pointers or functors). The equivalent mechanism in Java uses object or interface references.
- Through the use of stack-allocated objects, C++ supports scoped resource management, a technique used to automatically manage memory and other system resources that supports deterministic object destruction. Yet, scoped resource management in C++ cannot be guaranteed; it is only a design pattern, and hence relies on programmers' adherence. Java supports automatic memory management using garbage collection, but other system resources (windows, communication ports, threads) often have to be explicitly released if the garbage collector can

not determine they are no longer used.

- C++ features programmer-defined operator overloading which is not supported in Java. The only overloaded operators in Java are the "+" and "+=" operators, which concatenate strings as well as performing addition.
- Java features standard API support for reflection and dynamic loading of arbitrary new code.
- C++ supports static and dynamic linking of binary to manage the space required for binary and performance.
- Java has generics, whose main purpose is to provide type-safe containers. C++ has templates, which provide more extensive support for generic programming.
- Both Java and C++ distinguish between native types (these are also known as "fundamental" or "built-in" types) and user-defined types (these are also known as "compound" types). In Java, native types have value semantics only, and compound types have reference semantics only. In C++ all types have value semantics, but a reference can be created to any type, which will allow the object to be manipulated via reference semantics.
- C++ supports multiple inheritance of arbitrary classes. In Java a class can derive from only one class, but a class can implement multiple interfaces (in other words, it supports multiple inheritance of types, but only single inheritance of implementation).
- Java explicitly distinguishes between interfaces and classes. In C++ multiple inheritance and pure virtual functions make it possible to define classes that function almost like Java interfaces do, with a few small differences.
- Java has both language and standard library support for multi-threading. The synchronized keyword in Java provides simple and secure mutex locks to support multi-threaded applications, though synchronized sections have to be left in LIFO order. Java also provides robust and complex libraries for more advanced multi-threading synchronization. In C++ there is currently no defined memory model for multi-threading; however, third party libraries provide support roughly equivalent to that of Java; obvious difference being the non-uniformity of these C++ libraries.
- C++ methods can be declared as virtual functions, which means the method to be called is determined by the run-time type of the object. By default, methods in C++ are not virtual. In Java, methods are virtual by default, but can be made non-virtual by using the final keyword.
- C++ enumerations are primitive types and support conversion to and comparison with other integer types. Java enumerations are actually instances of a class (they extend java.lang.Enum<E>) and may therefore define constructors, fields, and methods as any other class.

Resource management

- Java offers automatic garbage collection. Memory management in C++ is usually done through constructors, destructors, and smart pointers. The C++ standard permits garbage collection, but does not require it; garbage collection is rarely used in practice. The enforced use of automatic garbage collection means that writing real-time software can be difficult in Java.
- C++ can allocate arbitrary blocks of memory. Java only allocates memory through object instantiation. (Note that in Java, the programmer can simulate allocation of arbitrary memory blocks by creating an array of bytes. Still, Java arrays are objects.)
- Java and C++ use different idioms for resource management. Java relies mainly on garbage collection, which can only reclaim memory and may be a last shot at other resources, while C++ relies mainly on the RAII (Resource Acquisition Is Initialization) idiom. This is reflected in several differences between the two languages:
  - In C++ it is common to allocate objects of compound types as local stack-bound variables which are destroyed when they go out of scope. In Java compound types are always allocated on the heap and collected by the garbage collector (except in virtual machines that use escape analysis to convert heap allocations to stack allocations).
  - C++ has destructors, while Java has finalizers. Both are invoked prior to an object's deallocation, but they differ significantly. A C++ object's destructor must be implicitly (in the case of stack-bound variables) or explicitly invoked to deallocate the object. The destructor executes synchronously just prior to the point in the program at which the object is deallocated. Synchronous, coordinated uninitialization and deallocation in C++ thus satisfy the RAII idiom. In Java, object deallocation is implicitly handled by the garbage collector. A Java object's finalizer is invoked asynchronously some time after it has been accessed for the last time and before it is actually deallocated, which may never happen. Very few objects require finalizers; a finalizer is only required by objects that must guarantee some clean up of the object state prior to deallocation — typically releasing resources external to the JVM. In Java safe synchronous deallocation of resources has to be performed explicitly using the try/finally construct.
  - In C++ it is possible to have a dangling pointer – a stale reference to an object that has already been deallocated; attempting to use a dangling pointer typically results in program failure. In Java, the garbage collector won't

destroy a referenced object.

- In C++ it is possible to have uninitialized primitive objects, Java enforces default initialization.
- In C++ it is possible to have an object that is allocated, but has no reachable reference to it. Such an unreachable object cannot be destroyed (deallocated), and results in a memory leak. In contrast, in Java an object will not be deallocated by the garbage collector *until* it becomes unreachable (by the user program). (Note: *weak references* are supported, which work with the Java garbage collector to allow for different *strengths* of reachability.) Garbage collection in Java prevents many memory leaks, but leaks are still possible under some circumstances.
- Java is more prone to leaking non-memory resources, while idiomatic C++ makes that much harder.

Libraries

- C++ provides cross-platform access to many features typically available in platform-specific libraries. Direct access from Java to native operating system and hardware functions requires the use of the Java Native Interface.

Runtime

- C++ is normally compiled directly to machine code which is then executed directly by the operating system. Java is normally compiled to byte-code which the Java virtual machine (JVM) then either interprets or JIT compiles to machine code and then executes.
- Due to its unconstrained expressiveness, low level C++ language features (e.g. unchecked array access, raw pointers, type punning) cannot be reliably checked at compile-time or without overhead at run-time. Related programming errors can lead to low-level buffer overflows and segmentation faults. The Standard Template Library provides higher-level abstractions (like vector, list and map) to help avoid such errors. In Java, low level errors either cannot occur or are detected by the JVM and reported to the application in the form of an exception.
- The Java language requires specific behavior in the case of an out-of-bounds array access, which generally requires bounds checking of array accesses. This eliminates a possible source of instability but usually at the cost of slowing down execution. In some cases, compiler analysis can prove a bounds check unnecessary and eliminate it. C++ has no required behavior for out-of-bounds access of native arrays, thus requiring no bounds checking for native arrays. C++ standard library collections like std::vector, however, offer optional bounds checking. In summary, Java arrays are "always safe; severely constrained; always have overhead" while C++ native arrays "have optional overhead; are completely unconstrained; are potentially unsafe."

Templates vs. Generics

Both C++ and Java provide facilities for generic programming, templates and generics, respectively. Although they were created to solve similar kinds of problems, and have similar syntax, they are actually quite different.

Miscellaneous

- Java and C++ use different techniques for splitting up code in multiple source files. Java uses a package system that dictates the file name and path for all program definitions. In Java, the compiler imports the executable class files. C++ uses a header file source code inclusion system for sharing declarations between source files.
- Compiled Java code files are generally smaller than code files in C++ as Java bytecode is usually more compact than native machine code and Java programs are never statically linked.
- C++ compilation features an additional textual preprocessing phase, while Java does not. Thus some users add a preprocessing phase to their build process for better support of conditional compilation.
- In both languages, arrays have a fixed size. In Java, arrays are first-class objects, while in C++ they are merely a continuous run of their base objects, often referred to using a pointer to their first element and an optional length. In Java, arrays are bounds-checked and know their length, while in C++ you can treat any subsequence as an array in its own right. Both C++ and Java provide container classes (**std::vector** and **java.util.ArrayList** respectively) which are resizable and store their size.
- Java's division and modulus operators are well defined to truncate to zero. C++ does not specify whether or not these operators truncate to zero or "truncate to -infinity". -3/2 will always be -1 in Java, but a C++ compiler may return either -1 or -2, depending on the platform. C99 defines division in the same fashion as Java. Both languages guarantee (where a and b are integer types) that (a/b)*b + (a%b) == a for all a and b (b != 0). The C++ version will sometimes be faster, as it is allowed to pick whichever truncation mode is native to the processor.
- The sizes of integer types is defined in Java (int is 32-bit, long is 64-bit), while in C++ the size of integers and pointers is compiler and ABI dependent within given constraints. Thus, carefully written C++ code can take advantage of the 64-bit processor's capabilities while still functioning properly on 32-bit processors. However, care must be taken to write the C++ program in a portable manner. In contrast, Java's fixed integer sizes mean that programmer error in this regard shouldn't be possible. This may incur a performance penalty since Java code cannot run using an

arbitrary processor's word size.

In addition to running a compiled Java program, computers running Java applications must also run the Java Virtual Machine JVM, while compiled C++ programs can be run without external applications. Early versions of Java were significantly outperformed by statically compiled languages such as C++. This is because the program statements of these two closely related languages may compile to a few machine instructions with C++, while compiling into several byte codes involving several machine instructions each when interpreted by a JVM. For example:

While C++ is faster than Java in most cases, there are several studies of mostly numerical benchmarks, which argue that Java could potentially outperform C++ in some circumstances,. However, it is widely recognized that numerical (micro-)benchmarks are not appropriate for evaluation of languages; two compilers with different performance on non-numerical sections of code may still be able to optimize numerical sections equally. If referring to a real world program, Java would suffer because of a number of reasons:

- All objects are allocated on the heap. For functions using small objects this can result in huge performance degradation as stack allocation, in contrast, costs essentially zero.
- Methods are by-default virtual. This increases memory usage as much as several times for small objects because of virtual function tables. Also, it induces a performance penalty, because a JIT compiler has to do additional optimization passes even for de-virtualization of small functions.
- A lot of casting required even using standard containers induces a performance penalty as it is necessary to walk through the entire inheritance hierarchy.
- A Virtual Java Machine increases memory usage even further, potentially reducing memory locality and increasing chances of cache misses.
- Lack of access to low level details does not allow the developer to better optimize the program where the compiler is unable to do so.

It is argued, however, that compared to Java, C++ also has a number of downsides:

- Pointers make optimization difficult since they may point to arbitrary data. However this is obsoleted as new compilers introduced *strict-aliasing* rule and because of support of the C99 keyword *restrict*.
- Java garbage collection may have better cache coherence than the usual usage of *malloc*/*new* for memory allocation, as its allocations are generally made sequentially. Nevertheless, arguments exist that both allocators equally fragment the heap and neither exhibits better cache locality.
- Run-time compilation can potentially use additional information available at run-time to optimise code more effectively, such as knowing what processor the code will be executed on. However this claim is effectively made obsolete as most state-of-the-art C++ compilers generate multiple code paths to employ the full computational abilities of the given system

Furthermore, it is arguable that time spent debugging more complex C++ code could just as easily be spent optimising existing Java code. Of course this is subject to other concerns such as how far it is possible to optimise bottleneck code in a given program. Ultimately, for processor-hungry cases such as video rendering, C++ has the direct access to hardware (being OS-native) and as such, will always be able to outperform Java given a particular hardware spec.

Proprietary control

C++ is not a trademark of any company or organization and is not owned by any individual. Java is a trademark of Sun Microsystems, which is now owned by Oracle.

The C++ language is defined by *ISO/IEC 14882*, an ISO standard, which is published by the *ISO/IEC JTC1/SC22/WG21* committee. The Java language is defined by the *Java Language Specification*, a book which is published by Sun (now Oracle).

Source (edited): "http://en.wikipedia.org/wiki/Comparison_of_Java_and_C%2B%2B"

Compatibility of C and C++

The C and C++ programming languages are closely related. C++ grew out of C, as it was designed to be source-and-link compatible with C. Due to this, C code is often developed with C++ IDEs, integrated with C++ code, and compiled in C++ compilers. While most C source code will compile as C++ code without any changes, certain language differences prevent C++ from being a strict superset of C.

Likewise, C++ introduces many features that are not available in C and in practice almost all code written in C++ is not conforming C code. This article, however, focuses on differences that cause conforming C code to be ill-formed C++ code, or to be conforming/well-formed in both languages but to behave differently in C and C++.

Bjarne Stroustrup, the creator of C++, has suggested that the incompatibilities between C and C++ should be reduced as much as possible in order to maximize inter-operability between the two languages. Others have argued that since C and C++ are two different languages, compatibility between them is useful but not vital; according to this camp, efforts to reduce incompatibility should not hinder attempts to improve each language in isolation. The official rationale for the 1999 C standard (C99) "endorse[d] the principle of maintaining the largest common subset" between C and C++ "while maintaining a distinction between them and allowing them to evolve separately," and stated that the authors were "content to let C++ be the big and ambitious language."

Several additions of C99 are not supported in C++ or conflict with C++ features, such as variadic macros, compound literals, designated initializers, variable-length arrays, and native complex-number types. The long long int datatype and restrict qualifier defined in C99 are not included in the current C++ standard, but some compilers such as the GNU Compiler Collection provide them as an extension. The long long datatype along with variadic templates, with which some functionality of variadic macros can be achieved, will be in the next C++ standard, C++0x. On the other hand, C99 has reduced some other incompatibilities by incorporating C++ features such as // comments and mixed declarations and code.

Constructs valid in C but not C++

One commonly encountered difference is that C allows a void* pointer to be assigned to any pointer type without a cast, whereas C++ does not; this idiom appears often in C code using malloc memory allocation. For example, the following is valid in C but not C++:

```
void* ptr;
int *i = ptr;      /* Implicit conversion
from void* to int* */
```

or similarly:

```
int *j = malloc(sizeof(int) * 5);    /*
Implicit conversion from void* to int*
*/
```

In order to make the code compile in both C and C++, one must use an explicit cast:

```
void* ptr;
int *i = (int *) ptr;
int *j = (int *) malloc(sizeof(int) * 5);
```

Another portability issue from C to C++ are the numerous additional keywords that C++ introduced. This makes C code that uses them as identifiers invalid in C++. For example:

```
struct template
{
   int new;
   struct template* class;
};
```

is valid C code, but is rejected by a C++ compiler, since the keywords "template", "new" and "class" are reserved.

C++ compilers prohibit using goto or switch from crossing an initialization, as in the following C99 code:

```
void fn(void)
{
 goto flack;
 int i = 1;
flack:
 ;
}
```

There are many other C syntaxes which are invalid or behave differently in C++ :

- The comma operator can result in an "l-value" (a quantity that can be used for the left-hand side of an assignment) in C++, but not in C.
- C does not allow a given typedef to be duplicated in the same scope, whereas C++ allows repeated typedefs.
- Enumeration constants (enum values) are always of type int in C, whereas they are distinct types in C++ and may have size different from that of int.
- C++ identifiers are not allowed to contain two or more consecutive underscores in any position. C identifiers are not allowed to start with two or more consecutive underscores, but may contain them in other positions.
- C++ also changes some C standard library functions to add additional const qualifiers, e.g. strchr returns char* in C and const char* in C++.
- In both C and C++ one can define nested struct types, but the scope is interpreted differently (in C++, a nested struct is defined only within the scope/namespace of the outer struct).
- Non-prototype ("K&R"-style) function declarations are not allowed in C++, although they have also been deprecated in C since 1990. Similarly, implicit function declarations (using functions that have not been declared) are not allowed in C++, but have also been deprecated in C since 1999.
- C allows struct, union, and enum types to be declared in function prototypes, whereas C++ does not.
- A struct, union, or enum declaration in C++ usually implies an implicit typedef of the same name, while in C it does not.
- In C, a function prototype without arguments, e.g. int foo();, implies that the parameters are unspecified. Therefore it is legal to call such a function with one or more arguments, e.g. foo(42, "hello world"). In contrast, in C++ a function prototype without arguments means that the function takes no arguments, and calling such a function with arguments is ill-formed. In C, the correct way to declare a function that takes no arguments is by using 'void', as in int foo(void);.
- C++ is more strict than C about pointer assignments that discard a const qualifier (e.g. assigning a const int* value to an int* variable): in C++ this is invalid and generates a compiler error (unless an explicit typecast is used), whereas in C this is allowed (although many compilers emit a warning).

Constructs that behave differently in C and C++

There are a few syntactical constructs that are valid in both C and C++, but produce different results in the two languages.

For example, character literals such as 'a' are of type int in C and of type char in C++, which means that sizeof 'a' will generally give different results in the two languages: in C++ it will be 1 in C it will be sizeof(int) which on architectures with 8 bit wide char will be at least 2. As another consequence of this type difference, in C 'a' will always be a signed expression, regardless of whether or not char is a signed or unsigned type, whereas for C++ this is compiler implementation specific.

The static keyword is used in C to restrict a function or global variable to file scope (internal linkage). This is also valid in C++, although C++ deprecates this usage in favor of anonymous namespaces (which are not available in C). Also, C++ implicitly treats any const global as file scope unless it is explicitly declared extern, unlike C in which extern is the default. Conversely, inline functions in C are of file scope whereas they have external linkage by default in C++.

Several of the other differences from the previous section can also be exploited to create code that compiles in both languages but behaves differently. For example, the following function will return different values in C and C++:

```
extern int T;

int size(void)
{
   struct T { int i; int j; };

   return sizeof(T);
   /* C:   return sizeof(int)
    * C++: return sizeof(struct T)
    */
}
```

This is due to C requiring struct in front of structure tags (and so sizeof(T) refers to the variable), but C++ allowing it to be omitted (and so sizeof(T) refers to the implicit typedef). Beware that the outcome is different when the extern declaration is placed inside the function: then the presence of an identifier with same name in the function scope inhibits the implicit typedef to take effect for C++, and the outcome for C and C++ would be the same. Observe also that the ambiguity in the example above is due to the use of the parenthesis with the sizeof operator. Using sizeof T would expect T to be an expression and not a type, and thus the example would not compile with C++.

Both C99 and C++ have a boolean type bool with constants true and false, but they behave differently. In C++, bool is a built-in type and a reserved keyword. In C99, a new keyword, _Bool, is introduced as the new boolean type. In many aspects, it behaves much like an unsigned int, but conversions from other integer types or pointers always constrained to 0 and 1. Other than for other unsigned types, and as one would expect for a boolean type, such a conversion is 0 if and only if the expression in question evaluates to 0 and it is 1 in all other cases. The header stdbool.h provides macros bool, true and false that are defined as _Bool, 1 and 0, respectively.

Linking C and C++ code

While C and C++ maintain a large degree of source compatibility, the object files their respective compilers produce can have important differences that manifest themselves when intermixing C and C++ code. Notably:

- C compilers do not name mangle symbols in the way that C++ compilers do.
- Depending on the compiler and architecture, it also may be the case that calling conventions differ between the two languages.

For these reasons, for C++ code to call a C function foo(), the C++ code must prototype foo() with extern "C". Likewise, for C code to call a C++ function bar(), the C++ code for bar() must be declared with extern "C".

A common practice for header files to maintain both C and C++ compatibility is to make its declaration be extern "C" for the scope of the header:

```
/* Header file foo.h */
#ifdef __cplusplus /* If this is a C++ compiler, use C linkage */
extern "C" {
#endif

/* These functions get C linkage */
void foo();

struct bar { /* ... */ };

#ifdef __cplusplus /* If this is a C++ compiler, end C linkage */
}
#endif
```

Differences between C and C++ linkage and calling conventions can also have subtle implications for code that uses function pointers. Some compilers will produce non-working code if a function pointer declared extern "C" points to a C++ function that is not declared extern "C".

For example, the following code:

```
void my_function();
extern "C" void foo(void (*fn_ptr)(void));

void bar()
{
  foo(my_function);
}
```

Using Sun Microsystems' C++ compiler, this produces the following warning:

```
$ CC -c test.cc
"test.cc", line 6: Warning
(Anachronism): Formal argument fn_ptr of type
extern "C" void(*)() in call to
foo(extern "C" void(*)()) is being passed
void(*)().
```

This is because my_function() is not declared with C linkage and calling conventions, but is being passed to the C function foo().

Source (edited): "http://en.wikipedia.org/wiki/Compatibility_of_C_and_C%2B%2B"

Concepts (C++)

In July 2009, the C++ standards committee decided to remove concepts from C++0x. This article documents concepts as they last appeared in a published working paper.

In the pending C++0x revision of the C++ programming language, **concepts** and the related notion of **axioms** were a proposed extension to C++'s template system, designed to improve compiler diagnostics and to allow programmers to codify in the program some formal properties of templates that they write. Incorporating these limited formal specifications into the program (in addition to improving code clarity) can guide some compiler optimizations, and can potentially help improve program reliability through the use of formal verification tools to check that the implementation and specification actually match.

In July 2009, the C++0x committee decided to remove concepts from the draft standard, as they are considered "not ready" for C++0x. There are unofficial plans to have the concepts back in the standard in some form, however no official decision has been made yet. A preliminary version of concepts for C++ has been implemented as ConceptGCC.

Motivation

C++ template classes and functions necessarily impose restrictions on the types that they take. For instance, the standard library containers require that the contained types be assignable. Unlike the dynamic polymorphism that class inheritance hierarchies exhibit, where a function that accepts an object of type Foo& can be passed any subtype of Foo, any class can be supplied as a template parameter so long as it supports all of the operations that users of actual instantiations upon that type use. In the case of the function, the requirement an argument must meet is clear (being a subtype of Foo), but in the case of a template the interface an object must meet is implicit in the implementation of that template. Concepts provide a mechanism for codifying the interface that a template parameter must meet. (See also: type class).

The primary motivation of the introduction of concepts is to improve the quality of compiler error messages. If a programmer attempts to use a type that does not provide the interface a template requires, the compiler will generate an error. However, such errors are often difficult to understand, especially for novices. There are two main reasons for this. First, error messages are often displayed with template parameters spelled out in full; this leads to extremely large error messages. On some compilers, simple errors can generate several kilobytes of error messages. Second, they often do not immediately refer to the actual location of the error. For example, if the programmer tries to construct a vector of objects that do not have a copy constructor, the first error almost always refers to the code within the vector class itself that attempts to copy construct its contents; the programmer must be skilled enough to understand that the real error was that the type doesn't support everything the vector class requires.

In an attempt to resolve this issue, it was proposed that C++0x add the language feature of *concepts*. Similar to how OOP uses a base-class to define restrictions on what a type can do, a concept is a named construct that specifies what a type must provide. Unlike OOP, however, the concept definition itself is not always associated explicitly with the type being passed into the template, but with the template definition itself:

```
template<LessThanComparable T>
 const T& min(const T &x, const T
&y)
 {
  return y < x ? y : x;
 }
```

Rather than using an arbitrary class or typename for the template type parameter, it uses LessThanComparable, which is a concept that was previously defined. If a type passed into the min template function does not satisfy the requirements of the LessThanComparable concept, then a compile error will result, telling the user that the type used to instantiate the template does not fit the LessThanComparable concept.

A more generalized form of the concept is as follows:

```
template< typename T> requires
LessThanComparable<T>
 const T& min(const T &x, const T
&y)
 {
  return y < x ? y : x;
 }
```

The keyword requires begins a list of *requirements*, which are specified by concept(s). In the requirement list, multiple concepts can be combined with boolean operation *negative*(!) and *logical-and*(&&) to form template constraint. Using the syntax of requires !LessThanComparable<T> if the user wishes to prevent the use of one particular template if the type matches the concept. This mechanism can be used in a way similar to template specialization. A general template would handle types with fewer features, explicitly disallowing the use of other, more feature-rich, concepts. And those concepts would have their own specializations that use those particular features to achieve greater performance or some other functionality. Another operation *logical-and* is also easy to use in the requirement list. For the type used in the template requires both assignment and copy-construct, just add requires Assignable<T>&&CopyConstructible<T>.

Concept definition

Concepts are defined as follows:

```
auto concept LessThanComparable<
typename T>
 {
  bool operator<(T, T);
 }
```

The keyword auto, in this instance, means that any type that supports the operations specified in the concept will be considered to support the concept. Without the use of the auto keyword, the type must use a concept map in order to declare itself as supporting the concept.

This concept says that any type that has an operator < that takes two objects of that type and returns a bool will be considered LessThanComparable. The operator need not be a free-function; it could be a member function of the type T.

Concepts can involve multiple objects as well. For example, concepts can express that a type is convertible from one type to another:

```
auto concept Convertible< typename
T, typename U>
{
 operator U(const T&);
}
```

In order to use this in a template, it must use a generalized form of concept usage:

```
template< typename U, typename T>
requires Convertible<T, U>
 U convert(const T& t)
 {
  return t;
 }
```

Concepts may be composed. For example, given a concept named Regular:

```
concept InputIterator< typename Iter,
typename Value>
{
 requires Regular<Iter>;
 Value operator*(const Iter&);
 Iter& operator++(Iter&);
 Iter operator++(Iter&, int);
}
```

The first template parameter to the InputIterator concept must conform to the Regular concept.

Concepts can also be derived from one another, like inheritance. Like in class inheritance, types that meet the requirements of the derived concept also meet the requirements of the base concept. It is defined as per class derivation:

```
concept ForwardIterator< typename
Iter, typename Value> :
InputIterator<Iter, Value>
{
 //Add other requirements here.
}
```

Typenames can also be associated with a concept. These impose the requirement that, in templates that use those concepts, these typenames are available:

```
concept InputIterator< typename Iter>
{
 typename value_type;
 typename reference;
 typename pointer;
 typename difference_type;
 requires Regular<Iter>;
 requires Convertible<reference, value
_type>;
 reference operator*(const Iter&); //
dereference
 Iter& operator++(Iter&); // pre-
increment
 Iter operator++(Iter&, int); // post-
increment
 // ...
}
```

Concept maps

Concept maps allow types to be explicitly bound to a concept. They also allow types to, where possible, adopt the syntax of a concept without changing the definition of the type. As an example:

```
concept_map InputIterator<char*>
{
 typedef char value_type;
 typedef char& reference;
 typedef char* pointer;
 typedef std::ptrdiff_t difference_type;
};
```

This map fills in the required typenames for the InputIterator concept when applied to char* types.

As an added degree of flexibility, concept maps themselves can be templated. The above example can be extended to all pointer types:

```
template< typename T> concept_map
InputIterator<T*>
{
 typedef T value_type;
 typedef T& reference;
 typedef T* pointer;
 typedef std::ptrdiff_t difference_type;
};
```

Further, concept maps can act as mini-types, with function definitions and other constructs commonly associated with classes:

```
concept Stack< typename X>
{
 typename value_type;
 void push(X&, const value_type&);
 void pop(X&);
 value_type top(const X&);
 bool empty(const X&);
};
```

```
template< typename T> concept_map
Stack<std::vector<T> >
{
 typedef T value_type;
 void push(std::vector<T>& v, const T
& x) { v.push_back(x); }
 void pop(std::vector<T>& v) { v.pop
_back(); }
 T top(const std::vector<T>& v) {
return v.back(); }
 bool empty(const std::vector<T>& v)
{ return v.empty(); }
};
```

This concept map allows templates that take types that implement the concept Stack to take a std::vector, remapping the function calls directly to the std::vector calls. Ultimately, this allows a pre-existing object to be converted, without touching the definition of the object, into an interface that a template function can utilize.

Finally, some requirements can be checked using static assertions. These can verify some requirements that templates need, but are really aimed at a different problem.

Axioms

Axioms are a facility pertaining to concepts supplied by C++0x to express the semantic properties of concepts. For example, the concept Semigroup can be defined with an axiom Associativity as

```
concept Semigroup< typename Op,
typename T> : CopyConstructible<T>
{
 T operator()(Op, T, T);

 axiom Associativity(Op op, T x, T y,
T z)
 {
  op(x, op(y, z)) == op(op(x, y), z);
 }
}
```

Compilers are allowed, but not required, to take advantage of the semantics specified by axioms to perform optimizations that possibly have side-effects on the observable behavior of the program, which are typically prohibited (with few exceptions such as copy constructor elision). In the above example, compilers may reassociate nested calls to operator() of type Op on several values of type T provided that there is a concept map for types Op and T to the concept Semigroup.

Axioms can also assist in software verification, software testing, and other program analyses and transformations.

Source (edited): "http://en.wikipedia.org/wiki/Concepts_(C%2B%2B)"

Copy constructor

A **copy constructor** is a special constructor in the C++ programming language creating a new object as a copy of an existing object. The first argument of such a constructor is a reference to an object of the same type as is being constructed (const or non-const), which might be followed by parameters of any type (all having default values).

Normally the compiler automatically creates a copy constructor for each class (known as a **default** copy constructor) but for special cases the programmer creates the copy constructor, known as a **user-defined** copy constructor. In such cases, the compiler does not create one.

A user-defined copy constructor is generally needed when an object owns pointers or non-shareable references, such as to a file, in which case a destructor and an assignment operator should also be written (see Rule of three).

Definition

Copying of objects is achieved by the use of a copy constructor and an assignment operator. A copy constructor has as its first parameter a (possibly const or volatile) reference to its own class type. It can have more arguments, but the rest must have default values associated with them. The following would be valid copy constructors for class X:

```
X (const X& copy_from_me);
X (X& copy_from_me);
X (const volatile X& copy_from_me);
X (volatile X& copy_from_me);
X (const X& copy_from_me, int = 10);
X (const X& copy_from_me, double =
1.0, int = 40);
```

The first one should be used unless there is a good reason to use one of the others. One of the differences between the first and the second is that temporaries can be copied with the first. For example:

```
X a = X();    // valid given X (const X
& copy_from_me) but not valid given
X (X& copy_from_me)
              // because the second wants a
non-const X&
              // to create a, the compiler
first creates a temporary by invoking
the default constructor
              // of X, then uses the copy
constructor to initialize a as a copy of
that temporary.
              // However, for some
compilers both the first and the second
actually work.
```

Another difference between them is the obvious:

```
X const a;
X b = a;      // valid given X (const X&
copy_from_me) but not valid given X
(X& copy_from_me)
              // because the second wants a
non-const X&
```

The X& form of the copy constructor is used when it is necessary to modify the copied object. This is very rare but it can be seen used in the standard library's std::auto_ptr. A reference must be provided:

```
X a;
X b = a;      // valid if any of the copy
constructors are defined
              // since a reference is being
passed.
```

The following are invalid copy constructors (Reason - copy_from_me is not passed as reference) :

```
X (X copy_from_me);
X (const X copy_from_me);
```

because the call to those constructors would require a copy as well, which would result in an infinitely recursive call.

The following cases may result in a call to a copy constructor:

- When an object is returned by value
- When an object is passed (to a function) by value as an argument
- When an object is thrown

- When an object is caught
- When an object is placed in a brace-enclosed initializer list

These cases are collectively called *copy-initialization* and are equivalent to: T x = a;

It is however, not guaranteed that a copy constructor will be called in these cases, because the C++ Standard allows the compiler to optimize the copy away in certain cases, one example being the return value optimization (sometimes referred to as RVO).

Operation

An object can be assigned value using one of the two techniques:

- Explicit assignment in an expression
- Initialization

Explicit assignment in an expression

```
Object A;
Object B;
A = B;      // translates as
Object::operator=(const Object&),
thus A.operator=(B) is called
            // (invoke simple copy, not
copy constructor!)
```

Initialization

An object can be initialized by any one of the following ways.

a. Through declaration

```
Object B = A; // translates as
Object::Object(const Object&) (invoke
copy constructor)
```

b. Through function arguments

```
type function (Object a);
```

c. Through function return value

```
Object a = function();
```

The copy constructor is used only for initializations, and does not apply to assignments where the assignment operator is used instead.

The implicit copy constructor of a class calls base copy constructors and copies its members by means appropriate to their type. If it is a class type, the copy constructor is called. If it is a scalar type, the built-in assignment operator is used. Finally, if it is an array, each element is copied in the manner appropriate to its type.

By using a user-defined copy constructor the programmer can define the behavior to be performed when an object is copied.

Examples

These examples illustrate how copy constructors work and why they are required sometimes.

Implicit copy constructor

Let us consider the following example.

```
//copy constructor
#include <iostream>

class Person {
public:
   int age;

   explicit Person (int age)
     : age (age) {}
};

int main()
{
   Person timmy (10);
   Person sally (15);

   Person timmy_clone = timmy;

   std::cout << timmy.age << " " <<
sally.age << " " << timmy_clone.age
<< std::endl;

   timmy.age = 23;

   std::cout << timmy.age << " " <<
sally.age << " " << timmy_clone.age
<< std::endl;

   return 0;
}
```

Output

```
10 15 10
23 15 10
```

As expected, *timmy* has been copied to the new object, *timmy_clone*. While *timmy's* age was changed, *timmy_clone's* age remained the same. This is because they are totally different objects.

The compiler has generated a copy constructor for us, and it could be written like this:

```
Person (const Person& copy)
  : age (copy.age) {}
```

So, when do we really need a user-defined copy constructor? The next section will explore that question.

User-defined copy constructor

Now, consider a very simple dynamic array class like the following:

```
#include <iostream>

class Array {
public:
   int size;
   int* data;

   explicit Array (int size)
      : size (size), data (new int[size])
{}

   ~Array()
   {
      delete[] data;
   }
};

int main()
{
   Array first (20);
   first.data[0] = 25;

   {
      Array copy = first;

      std::cout << first.data[0] << " "
<< copy.data[0] << std::endl;

   }  // (1)

   first.data[0] = 10;   // (2)

   return 0;
}
```

Output

```
25 25
```

Segmentation fault

Since we did not specify a copy constructor, the compiler generated one for us. The generated constructor would look something like:

```
Array (const Array& copy)
  : size (copy.size), data (copy.data) {}
```

The problem with this constructor is that it performs a shallow copy of the *data* pointer. It only copies the address of the original data member; this means they both share a pointer to the same chunk of memory, which is not what we want. When the program reaches line **(1)**, *copy's* destructor gets called (because objects on the stack are destroyed automatically when their scope ends). *Array's* destructor deletes the *data* array of the original, therefore when it deleted *copy's* data, because they share the same pointer, it also deleted *first's* data. Line **(2)** now accesses invalid data and writes to it! This produces the infamous segmentation fault.

If we write our own copy constructor that performs a *deep copy* then this problem goes away.

```
Array(const Array& copy)
  : size(copy.size), data(new int[copy.
size])
{
  std::copy(copy.data, copy.data +
copy.size, data);    // #include
<algorithm> for std::copy
}
```

Here, we are creating a new **int** array and copying the contents to it. Now, *copy's* destructor only deletes its data and not *first's* data as well. Line **(2)** will not produce a segmentation fault anymore.

Instead of doing a deep copy right away, there are some optimization strategies that can be used. These allow you to safely share the same data between several objects, thus saving space. The copy on write strategy makes a copy of the data only when it is written to. Reference counting keeps the count of how many objects are referencing the data, and will delete it only when this count reaches zero (e.g. boost::shared_ptr).

Copy constructors and templates

Contrary to expectations, a template copy constructor is not a user-defined copy constructor. Thus it is not enough to just have:

```
template <typename A> Array::Array
(const A& copy)
  : size (copy.size()), data (new
int[copy.size()])
{
  std::copy (copy.begin(), copy.end(),
data);
}
```

(Note that the type of A can be Array.) A user-defined, non-template copy constructor must also be provided for construction of Array from Array.

Explicit copy constructor

An explicit copy constructor is one that is declared explicit by using the **explicit** keyword. For example:

```
explicit X (const X& copy_from_me);
```

It is used to prevent copying of objects at function calls or with the copy-initialization syntax.

Source (edited): "http://en.wikipedia.org/wiki/Copy_constructor"

Copy elision

In C++ computer programming, **copy elision** refers to a compiler optimization technique that eliminates unnecessary copying of objects. The C++ language standard generally allows implementations to perform any optimization, as long as the resulting program's observable behavior is the same *as if* the program was executed exactly as mandated by the standard.

The standard also describes a few situations where copying can be eliminated even if this would alter the program's behavior, the most common being the return value optimization. Another case is described in section 12.8, paragraph 15 of the C++ standard, namely when a temporary object of class type is copied to an object of the same type. This is also a very widely implemented optimization. As a result, *copy-initialization* is usually equivalent to *direct-initialization* in terms of performance, but not in semantics; *copy-initialization* still requires an accessible copy constructor. The optimization can not be applied to a temporary object that has been bound to a reference. Example:

```
int n = 0;
struct C {
  C(int) {}
  C(const C&) { ++n; } // the copy
constructor has a visible side effect
};                   // it modifies an object
with static storage duration

int main() {
  C c1(42); // direct-initialization, calls
C::C(42)
  C c2 = 42; // copy-initialization, calls
C::C(42) _or_ C::C( C(42) )

  return n; // returns either 0 or 1,
depending on whether the copy was
elided
}
```

The standard also mentions that a similar optimization may be applied to objects being thrown and caught, but it is unclear whether the optimization applies to both the copy from the thrown object to the *exception object*, and the copy from the *exception object* to the object declared in the *exception-declaration* of the *catch clause*. It is also unclear whether this optimization only applies to temporary objects, or named objects as well. Given the following source code:

```
#include <iostream>

struct C {
  C() {}
  C(const C&) { std::cout << "Hello
World!\n"; }
};

void f() {
  C c;
  throw c; // copying the named object
c into the exception object.
}         // It is unclear whether this
copy may be elided.

int main() {
  try {
    f();
  }
  catch(C c) {  // copying the exception
object into the temporary in the
exception declaration.
  }          // It is also unclear whether
this copy may be elided.
}
```

A conforming compiler should therefore produce a program that prints "Hello World!" twice. In the upcoming C++ standard (C++0x), the issues have been addressed, essentially allowing both the copy from the named object to the exception object, and the copy into the object declared in the exception handler to be elided.

Source (edited): "http://en.wikipedia.org/wiki/Copy_elision"

Curiously recurring template pattern

The **curiously recurring template pattern** (**CRTP**) is a C++ idiom in which a class X derives from a class template instantiation using X itself as template argument. The name of this idiom was coined by Jim Coplien, who had observed it in some of the earliest C++ template code.

General form

```
// The Curiously Recurring Template
Pattern (CRTP)
template <typename T>
struct base
{
    // ...
};
struct derived : base<derived>
{
    // ...
};
```

Some use cases for this pattern are static polymorphism, and other metaprogramming techniques such as those described by Andrei Alexandrescu in *Modern C++ Design*.

Static polymorphism

Typically, the base class template will take advantage of the fact that member function bodies (definitions) are not instantiated until long after their declarations, and will use members of the derived class within its own member functions, via the use of a cast in the case of multiple inheritance e.g.:

```
template <class Derived>
struct Base
{
    void interface()
    {
        // ...
        static_cast<Derived*>(this)-
>implementation();
        // ...
    }

    static void static_func()
    {
        // ...
        Derived::static_sub_func();
        // ...
    }
};

struct Derived : Base<Derived>
{
    void implementation();
    static void static_sub_func();
};
```

This technique achieves a similar effect

to the use of virtual functions, without the costs (and some flexibility) of dynamic polymorphism. This particular use of the CRTP has been called "simulated dynamic binding" by some. This pattern is used extensively in the Windows ATL and WTL libraries.

To elaborate on the above example, consider a base class with **no virtual functions**. Whenever the base class calls another member function, it will always call its own base class functions. When we derive a class from this base class, we inherit all the member variables and member functions that weren't overridden (no constructors or destructors). If the derived class calls an inherited function that then calls another member function, that function will never call any derived or overridden member functions in the derived class.

However, if base class member functions use CRTP for all member function calls, the overridden functions in the derived class will be selected at compile time. This effectively emulates the virtual function call system at compile time without the costs in size or function call overhead (VTBL structures, and method lookups, multiple-inheritance VTBL machinery) at the disadvantage of not being able to make this choice at runtime.

Object counter

The main purpose of an object counter is retrieving statistics of object creation and destruction for a given class. This can be easily solved using CRTP:

```
template <typename T>
struct counter
{
  static int objects_created;
  static int objects_alive;

  counter()
  {
    ++objects_created;
    ++objects_alive;
  }
protected:
  ~counter() // objects should never be
removed through pointers of this type
  {
    --objects_alive;
  }
};
template <typename T> int
counter<T>::objects_created( 0 );
template <typename T> int
counter<T>::objects_alive( 0 );

class X : counter<X>
{
  // ...
};

class Y : counter<Y>
{
  // ...
};
```

Each time an object of class X is created, the constructor of counter<X> is called, incrementing both the created and alive count. Each time an object of class X is destroyed, the alive count is decremented. It is important to note that counter<X> and counter<Y> are two separate classes and this is why they will keep separate counts of X's and Y's. In this example of CRTP, this distinction of classes is the only use of the template parameter (T in counter<T>) and the reason why we cannot use a simple un-templated base class.

Polymorphic copy construction

When using polymorphism, one quite often needs to create copies of objects by the base class pointer. A commonly used idiom for this is adding a virtual clone function that is defined in every derived class. The CRTP pattern can be used to avoid having to duplicate that function or other similar functions in every derived class.

```
// Base class has a pure virtual function
for cloning
class Shape {
public:
  virtual ~Shape() {}
  virtual Shape *clone() const = 0;
};
// This CRTP class implements clone()
for Derived
template <typename Derived> class
Shape_CRTP: public Shape {
public:
  Shape *clone() const {
    return new Derived(static
_cast<Derived const&>(*this));
  }
};
// Every derived class inherits from
Shape_CRTP instead of Shape
class Square: public Shape
_CRTP<Square> {};
class Circle: public Shape
_CRTP<Circle> {};
```

This allows obtaining copies of squares, circles or any other shapes by shapePtr->clone().

In other languages

The CRTP makes an appearance in the Java programming language standard library where the Enum class is defined as Enum<T extends Enum<T>>.

Source (edited): "http://en.wikipedia.org/wiki/Curiously_recurring_template_pattern"

Database Management Library

DBL - Database Management Library is a RDBMS contained in a C++ programming library. The DBL source code is available under the terms of the GNU General Public License.

DBL was developed as a holidays programming project, and it was completely developed within two weeks.

It aims at being easy and simple for C++ programmers to use.

Design

DBL is a library and becomes an integral part of the application program. Unlike client–server database management systems that are standalone process with which the application program communicates. The application softwares uses DBL's functionality through function calls.

Sample Programs

Creating a simple database

This is a basic program that creates a simple database. However, as this task must be done usually once, it can be done by the DBL Command-Line Interface.

```
#include "dbl.h"

int main()
{
   path( "D:\\" ); //set the path to the
folder where the files will be stored

   database db("mydatabase");
//mydatabase is the name of the
database
   db.new_tab("customer"); //create a
new table called customer in the
database

   write(db); //write the database
structure into a file

   char pkey = 1;
   table *tab = db.get_tab("customer");
//get the table customer from the
database
   tab->add_col("cod", INTEGER, 1,
pkey); //add a column called cod to
the table customer
   tab->add_col("name",
CHARACTER, 32); //add a column
called name to the table customer
   tab->add_col("brithdate",
INTEGER, 3);
   tab->add_col("sex", CHARACTER,
1);
   tab->add_col("phone", INTEGER,
1);
   tab->set_structure();
   write(*tab); //write the table
structure into files
   create_data_file(*tab); //create the
data file of the table customer

   return 0;
}
```

Inserting data into a table

This is a basic program that inserts a new record in the table.

```
#include "dbl.h"

int main()
{
   path( "D:\\" ); //set the path to the
folder where the files will be stored

   database db("mydatabase");
//mydatabase is the name of the
database
   read(db); //load the database
structure

   table *tab = db.get_tab("customer");
//get the table customer from the
database
   row r( tab->new_row() ); //get a row
with the structure of the table customer

   int cod = 31415;
   char name[32] = "Charles";
   int birthdate[3] = {27, 6, 2010};
   char sex = 'm';
   int phone = 88123456;

   //set the values stored by the row
   r.set(0, &cod);
   r.set(1, name);
   r.set(2, birthdate);
   r.set(3, &sex);
   r.set(4, &phone);

   int i = num_row(*tab); //get the
number of rows in the data file

   //write the row into the data file of
the table customer,
   //where i is the index of the new
record
   write(*tab, r, i );

   return 0;
}
```

The Library Structure

The Class database

This class stores the database name and its tables. The main functions are:

char *name(); //get the database name
char *name(char *dbname); //set the database name
void new_tab(char *tabname); //create a new table
table *get_tab(char *tabname); //return the pointer to the table

Useful functions that use the class database are:

void write(database &db); //write the database structure into a file
friend void read(database &db); //read the database structure from a file
friend void del(database &db); //delete the database and its tables files
friend void print(database &db); //print the database on the screen

The Class table

This class stores the table name and its structure, the columns of the table. The main functions are:

char *name(); //get the table name
char *name(char *dbname); //set the table name
void add_col(column &c); //add a new column to the table
void add_col(char *col_name, char col_type, int col_len=1, char pkey=0);
column *get_col(int idx); //get the column by its index
column *get_col(char *name); //get the column by its name
int num_col(); //get the number of columns in the table

//finish the structure of the table.
//This function must be called after adding all columns or after reading the structure of the table from a file
void set_structure();

row new_row(); //get a new row with the table structure

Useful functions that use the class table are:

void write(table &t); //write the table structure into a file
void read(table &t); //read the table structure from a file
friend void del(table &t); //delete the table files, header and data files
void print(table &t); //print the table on the screen
friend std::ostream &operator<<(std::ostream &o, table &t); //print the table structure
int num_row(table &t); //get the number of rows in the data file of the table

The Class row

This class stores the columns of the table and the data to be stored in the data file. The main functions are:

void set(int idx, storage &s); //set the storage of a column by its index
void set(int idx, void* v); //set the value to be stored in a column by its index
storage *get(int idx); //get the storage from the a column by its index

Useful functions that use the class row are:

void write(table &t, row &r, int idx); //write the data in the data file of the table
void read(table &t, row &r, int idx); //read the data from the data file of the table
void del(char *file, table &t, int idx); //delete the data from the data file of the table

The Class storage

This class stores the column and a value for that column. The main functions are:

char *value(); //get the value being stored by the object
void value(void *val); //set the value to be stored
void value(char *val); //set the value to be stored, a C-style string and all functions of the class column.

Useful functions that use the class storage are:

int get_int(storage &s); //get the integer being stored
char get_char(storage &s); //get the char being stored
bool get_bool(storage &s); //get the bool being stored
float get_float(storage &s); //get the float being stored
double get_double(storage &s); //get the double being stored

The Class column

This class stores the name and the structure of a column. The main functions are:

char *name(); //get the name of the column
char *name(char *n); //set the name of the column
char type(); //get the type of the column
char type(char t); //set the type of the column
int length(); //get the length of the array that the column can hold
int length(int len); //set the length of the array that the column can hold, len>0
void pkey(char b); //set if the column is the primary key or not (0 is false, 1 is true)
char pkey(); //get if the column is the primary key or not
int total_size(); //get the total size, in bytes, that the column can hold

The Class index

This class stores the indexes of a table. The main functions are:

int seek(void *val); //look for a value in the indexes
int seek(char *val); //look for a C-style string in the indexes

Useful functions that use the class index are:

void write(table &t, index &idx); //write the indexes of a table into a file
void read(index &idx); //read the indexes from a file

DBL Command-Line Interface

By the DBL Command-Line Interface program one can create a database, create a table and add columns to this table, besides others operations such as printing.

Source (edited): "http://en.wikipedia.org/wiki/Database_Management_Library"

David Abrahams (computer programmer)

David Abrahams is a computer programmer and author. He is most well-known for his activities related to the C ++ programming language. In particular his contributions to the language include the delineating of a theory of exceptions, sitting on the C++ Standards Committee, being a founding member of Boost and co-authoring a book on the subject of template meta-programming.

Abrahams became a member of the C++ Standards Committee in 1996. During the standardization process that resulted in the first ANSI standard C++ - in 1998 - Abrahams was a principal driving force behind detailing the exception safety of the C++ Standard Library. Many of the functions and methods of the standard are specified with one of three guarantees. Together these have become known as the Abrahams guarantees.

Following the standardization, Abrahams became one of the founding members of boost.org, a community group founded in order to provide reusable C++ libraries. Abrahams has written several of the libraries and assisted in the development of others. As of 2007, he still actively contributes to the group. Abrahams is also the principal member of Boost Consulting, a company that offers software development and training courses with a heavy bias towards using the Boost C++ Libraries.

Source (edited): "http://en.wikipedia.org/wiki/David_Abrahams_(computer_programmer)"

decltype

In the C++ programming language, **decltype** is an operator for querying the type of an expression. It will be included in the upcoming version of the C++ Standard, often referred to as C++0x. Its primary intended use is in generic programming, where it is often difficult, or even impossible, to express types that depend on template parameters.

As generic programming techniques became increasingly popular throughout the 1990s, the need for a type-deduction mechanism was recognized. Many compiler vendors implemented their own versions of the operator, typically called typeof, and some portable implementations with limited functionality, based on existing language features were developed. In 2002, Bjarne Stroustrup proposed that a standardized version of the operator be added to the C++ language, and suggested the name "decltype", to reflect that the operator would yield the "declared type" of an expression.

decltype's semantics were designed to cater to both generic library writers and novice programmers. In general, the deduced type matches the type of the object or function exactly as declared in the source code. Like the sizeof operator, decltype's operand is not evaluated.

Motivation

With the introduction of templates into the C++ programming language, and the advent of generic programming techniques pioneered by the Standard Template Library, the need for a mechanism for obtaining the type of an expression, commonly referred to as typeof, was recognized. In generic programming, it is often difficult or impossible to express types that depend on template parameters, in particular the return type of function template instantiations.

Many vendors provide the typeof operator as a compiler extension. As early as 1997, before C++ was fully standardized, Brian Parker proposed a portable solution based on the sizeof operator. His work was expanded on by Bill Gibbons, who concluded that the technique had several limitations and was generally less powerful than an actual typeof mechanism. In an October 2000 article of *Dr. Dobb's Journal*, Andrei Alexandrescu remarked that "[h]aving a typeof would make much template code easier to write and understand." He also noted that "typeof and sizeof share the same backend, because sizeof has to compute the type anyway." Andrew Koenig and Barbara E. Moo also recognized the usefulness of a built-in typeof facility, with the caveat that "using it often invites subtle programming errors, and there are some problems that it cannot solve." They characterized the use of type conventions, like the typedefs provided by the Standard Template Library, as a more powerful and general technique. However, Steve Dewhurst argued that such conventions are "costly to design and promulgate", and that it would be "much easier to ... simply extract the type of the expression."

In 2002, Bjarne Stroustrup suggested extending the C++ language with mechanisms for querying the type of an expression, and initializing objects without specifying the type. Stroustrup observed that the reference-dropping semantics offered by the typeof operator provided by the GCC and EDG compilers could be problematic. Conversely, an operator returning a reference type based on the lvalue-ness of the expression was deemed too confusing. The initial proposal to the C++ standards committee outlined a combination of the two variants; the operator would return a reference type only if the declared type of the expression included a reference. To emphasize that the deduced type would reflect the "declared type" of the expression, the operator was proposed to be named decltype.

One of the cited main motivations for the decltype proposal, was the ability to write perfect forwarding function templates. It is sometimes desirable to write a generic forwarding function that returns the same type as the wrapped function, regardless of the type it is instantiated with. Without decltype, it is not generally possible to accomplish this. An example, which also utilizes the proposed *trailing-return-type*:

```
int& foo(int& i);
float foo(float& f);

template <class T> auto transparent
_forwarder(T& t) −> decltype(foo(t)) {
  return foo(t);
}
```

decltype is essential here because it preserves the information about whether the wrapped function returns a reference type.

Semantics

Similarly to the sizeof operator, the operand of decltype is unevaluated. Informally, the type returned by decltype(e) is deduced as follows:

- If the expression e refers to a variable in local or namespace scope, a static member variable or a function parameter, then the result is that variable's or parameter's *declared type*
- If e is a function call or an overloaded operator invocation, decltype(e) denotes the *declared return type* of that function
- Otherwise, if e is an lvalue, decltype(e) is T&, where T is the type of e; if e is an rvalue, the result is T

These semantics were designed to fulfill the needs of generic library writers, while at the same time being intuitive for novice programmers, because the return type of decltype always matches the type of the object or function exactly as declared in the source code. More formally, Rule 1 applies to unparenthesized *id-expression*s and class member access expressions. For function calls, the deduced type is the return type of the statically chosen function, as determined by the rules for overload resolution. Example:

```
const int&& foo();
int i;
struct A { double x; };
const A* a = new A();
decltype(foo()) x1; // type is const int&
&
decltype(i) x2; // type is int
decltype(a->x) x3; // type is double
decltype((a->x)) x4; // type is const
double&
```

The reason for the difference between the latter two invocations of decltype is that the parenthesized expression (a->x) is neither an *id-expression* nor a member access expression, and therefore does not denote a named object. Because the expression is an lvalue, its deduced type is "reference to the type of the expression", or const double&.

In December 2008, a concern was raised to the committee by Jaakko Järvi over the inability to use decltype to form a *qualified-id*, which is inconsistent with the intent that decltype(e) should be treated "as if it were a *typedef-name*". While commenting on the formal Committee Draft for C++0x, the Japanese ISO member body noted that "a scope operator(::) cannot be applied to decltype, but it should be. It would be useful in the case to obtain member type(nested-type) from an instance as follows":

```
vector<int> v;
decltype(v)::value_type i = 0; // int i =
0;
```

This, and similar issues pertaining to the wording inhibiting the use of decltype in the declaration of a derived class and in a destructor call, were addressed by David Vandevoorde, and voted into the working paper in March 2010.

Availability

decltype is slated for inclusion in the next version of the C++ Language Standard, informally referred to as C++0x. It is provided by a number of compilers as an extension. Microsoft's Visual C++ 2010 compiler provides a decltype operator that closely mimics the semantics as described in the standards committee proposal. It can be used with both managed and native code. The documentation states that it is "useful primarily to developers who write template libraries." decltype was added to the mainline of the GCC C++ compiler in version 4.3, released on March 5, 2008. The operator is also present in Codegear's C++ Builder 2009, the Intel C++ Compiler, and Clang.

Source (edited): "http://en.wikipedia.org/wiki/Decltype"

delete (C++)

In the C++ programming language, the delete operator calls the destructor of the given argument, and returns memory allocated by new back to the heap. A call to delete must be made for every call to new to avoid a memory leak. After calling delete the memory object pointed to is invalid and should no longer be used. Many programmers assign 0 (null pointer) to pointers after using delete to help minimize programming errors. Note, however, that deleting a null pointer has no effect (if the deallocation function is one supplied in the standard library), so it is not necessary to check for a null pointer before calling delete.

Example code snippet:

```
int *p_var = 0;    // new pointer declared
p_var = new int;     // memory dynamically allocated

/* .......
other code
........*/

delete p_var;          // memory freed up
p_var = 0;         // pointer changed to 0 (null pointer)
```

Arrays allocated with new [] can be similarly deallocated with delete []:

```
int size = 10;
int *p_var = 0;     // new pointer declared
p_var = new int [size];// memory dynamically allocated

/* .......
other code
........*/

delete [] p_var;       // memory freed up
p_var = 0;          // pointer changed to 0
```

Arrays, allocated with new[], must be deallocated with delete[], since the layout of arrays, allocated with new[] is implementation defined, and possibly not compatible with new. For example, in order to properly perform object destruction at delete[], some implementations of new[] embed the number of allocated objects into the beginning of the allocated memory chunk, and return pointer to the remaining part of the array..

The delete operator (user defined) is different from operator delete. The delete operator may call operator delete to free up memory.

Source (edited): "http://en.wikipedia.org/wiki/Delete_(C%2B%2B)"

Dev-C++

Dev-C++ is a free integrated development environment (IDE) distributed under the GNU General Public License for programming in C and C++. It is bundled with MinGW, a free compiler. The IDE is written in Delphi.

The project is hosted by SourceForge. Dev-C++ was originally developed by programmer Colin Laplace. Dev-C++ runs exclusively on Microsoft Windows.

Bloodshed Dev-C++ is a full-featured Integrated Development Environment (IDE) for the C and C++ programming languages. It uses the MinGW port of the GCC as its compiler. Dev-C++ can also be used in combination with Cygwin or any other GCC-based compiler.

One additional aspect of Dev-C++ is its use of DevPaks, packaged extensions on the programming environment with additional libraries, templates, and utilities. DevPaks often contain, but are not limited to, GUI utilities, including popular toolkits such as GTK+, wxWidgets, and FLTK. Other DevPaks include libraries for more advanced function use.

Dev-C++ is generally considered a Windows-only program, but there were attempts to create a Linux version.

Devpaks

Users of Dev-C++ can download additional libraries, or packages of code that increase the scope and functionality of Dev-C++, such as graphics, compression, animation, sound support and many more. Users can create Devpaks and host them for free on the site. Also, they are not limited to use with Dev C++. The site says "A typical devpak will work with any MinGW distribution (with any IDE for MinGW)".

Development status

The project is no longer noticeably active, with no news posted nor any updated versions released since February 22, 2005. In a 2006 forum post, lead developer Colin Laplace stated that he was busy with real-life issues and did not have time to continue development of Dev-C++. However there is a development team that has taken the Dev-C++ IDE and added new features such as support for multiple compilers and a RAD designer for wxWidgets applications. This IDE can be found under the name wxDev-C++.

Source (edited): "http://en.wikipedia.org/wiki/Dev-C%2B%2B"

Dominance (C++)

In the C++ programming language, **dominance** implies a specific behaviour of symbol disambiguation in virtual inheritance. Consider the following example:

```
class Parent
{
public:
   virtual void function();
};

class Child1 : public virtual Parent
{
public:
   void function();
};

class Child2 : public virtual Parent
{
};

class Grandchild : public Child1,
public Child2
{
public:
  Grandchild()
   {
     function();
   }
};
```

In the Grandchild call to function(), Child1::function is implied, because Child1 is derived from Parent and thus Child1::function "dominates" Parent::function.

Source (edited): "http://en.wikipedia.org/wiki/Dominance_(C%2B%2B)"

dynamic_cast

In the C++ programming language, the **dynamic_cast** operator is a part of the run-time type information (RTTI) system that performs a typecast. Unlike an ordinary C-style typecast, a type safety check is performed at runtime, and if the types are not compatible, an exception will be thrown (when dealing with references) or a null pointer will be returned (when dealing with pointers). In this regard, dynamic_cast behaves like a Java typecast.

Example code

Suppose some function takes an object of type A as its argument, and wishes to perform some additional operation if the object passed is an instance of B, a subclass of A. This can be accomplished using dynamic_cast as follows.

```
#include <typeinfo> // For std::bad
_cast
#include <iostream> // For std::cerr,
etc.

class A
{
public:
    // Since RTTI is included in the
virtual method table there should be at
least one virtual function.
    virtual void foo();

    // other members...
};

class B : public A
{
public:
    void methodSpecificToB();

    // other members.
};

void my_function(A& my_a)
{
    try
    {
        B& my_b = dynamic_cast<B
&>(my_a);
        my_b.methodSpecificToB();
    }
    catch (const std::bad_cast& e)
    {
        std::cerr << e.what() <<
std::endl;
        std::cerr << "This object is
not of type B" << std::endl;
    }
}
```

A similar version of my_function can be written with pointers instead of references:

```
void my_function(A* my_a)
{
    B* my_b = dynamic
_cast<B*>(my_a);

    if (my_b != NULL)
        my_b-
>methodSpecificToB();
    else
        std::cerr << "This object is
not of type B" << std::endl;


}
```

Source (edited): "http://en.wikipedia.org/wiki/Dynamic_cast"

E. Balagurusamy

Dr.E. BALAGURUSAMY

Dr. E. Balagurusamy, former Vice Chancellor of Anna University, Chennai. He is currently Member of Union Public Service Commission, New Delhi. He is a teacher, trainer, and consultant management in the fields of Information Technology add management. He holds Master of Engineering (Hons) in Electrical Engineering and a Ph. D in System Engineering from the Indian Institute of Technology Roorkee. His main areas of interest include Object-Oriented Software Engineering, Electronic business, Technology Management, Business Process Re-engineering, and Total Quality management. He is most well-known for his activities related to the C++ programming language and is one of the world's foremost C++ experts.

Source (edited): "http://en.wikipedia.org/wiki/E._Balagurusamy"

Edison Design Group

The **Edison Design Group** (**EDG**) is a company that makes compiler frontends (preprocessing and parsing). Their frontends are widely used in commercially available compilers and code analysis tools. Users include the Intel C++ compiler, SGI MIPSpro, The Portland Group, and Comeau C++. They are widely known for having the first, and likely only, frontend to implement the export keyword of C++.

Edison was founded by MIT graduate Steve Adamczyk. Other employees include John Spicer and Daveed Vandevoorde.

Source (edited): "http://en.wikipedia.org/wiki/Edison_Design_Group"

Erase-remove idiom

The **erase-remove idiom** is a common C++ technique to eliminate elements that fulfill a certain criterion from a C++ Standard Library container.

Motivation

A common programming task is remove all elements that have a certain value or fulfill a certain criterion from a collection. In C++, this could be achieved using a hand-written loop. It is, however, preferred to use an algorithm from the C++ Standard Library for such tasks.

The algorithms library provides the remove and remove_if algorithms for this. Because these algorithms operate on a range of elements denoted by two forward iterators, they have no knowledge of the underlying container or collection. Thus, the elements are not actually removed from the range, merely moved to the end. When all the removed elements are at the end of the range, remove returns an iterator pointing one past the last unremoved element.

To actually eliminate elements from the container, remove is combined with the container's erase member function, hence the name "erase-remove idiom".

Example

```
#include <vector> // the general-
purpose vector container
#include <algorithm> // remove and
remove_if

bool is_odd(int i) // unary predicate
returning true if and only if the
argument is odd
{
  return i % 2;
}
bool is_even(int i) // unary predicate
returning true if and only if the
argument is even
{
  return !is_odd(i);
}

int main()
{
  using namespace std;
  int elements[] = {0, 1, 2, 3, 4, 5, 6, 7,
8, 9 };
  // create a vector that holds the
numbers from 0-9.
  vector<int> v(elements, elements +
10);

  // use the erase-remove idiom to
remove all elements with the value 5
  v.erase(remove(v.begin(), v.end(), 5),
v.end());

  // use the erase-remove idiom to
remove all odd numbers
  v.erase( remove_if(v.begin(), v.end(),
is_odd), v.end() );

  // use the erase-remove idiom to
remove all even numbers
  v.erase( remove_if(v.begin(), v.end(),
is_even), v.end() );
}
```

Source (edited): "http://en.wikipedia.org/wiki/Erase-remove_idiom"

Exception guarantees

Exception guarantees, also known as the **Abrahams guarantees** after David Abrahams, who formalized the guidelines, are a set of contractual guidelines that class library implementors and clients use when reasoning about exception safety in C++ programs.

The rules apply to class implementations (components) in the presence of exceptions; they are as follows:

- The strong guarantee: that the operation has either completed successfully or thrown an exception, leaving the program state exactly as it was before the operation started.
- The basic guarantee: that the invariants of the component are preserved, and no resources are

leaked. Often referred to as the weak guarantee, because following an exception the system is left in a safe, but unknown, state.

- The no-throw guarantee: that the operation will not throw an exception.

Code that doesn't follow at least one of the above rules is called *exception unsafe*.

Source (edited): "http://en.wikipedia.org/wiki/Exception_guarantees"

Expression templates

Expression templates is a C++ template metaprogramming technique in which templates are used to represent part of an expression. Typically, the template itself represents a particular type of operation, while the parameters represent the operation to which the operation applies. The expression template can then be evaluated at a later time, or passed to a function. The technique was invented independently by Todd Veldhuizen and David Vandevoorde.

For example, consider a library representing vectors with a class Vec. It is natural to want to overload operator- and operator* so you could write Vec x = alpha*(u - v); where alpha is a scalar and u and v are Vecs. A naive implementation would have operator- and operator* return Vecs. However, then the above expression would mean creating a temporary for u-v then another temporary for alpha times that first temporary, then assigning that to x.

Expression templates delay evaluation so the expression Vec x = alpha*(u-v); essentially generates at compile time a new Vec constructor taking a scalar and two Vecs as follows (using the curiously recurring template pattern as is used by Boost.uBLAS):

```
#include <vector>
#include <cassert>

template <typename E>
// A CRTP base class for Vecs with a
size and indexing:
class VecExpression {
public:
  typename E::size_type size() const {
return static_cast<E const&>(*this).
size(); }
  typename E::value_type
operator[](size_type i) const { return
static_cast<E const&>(*this)[i]; }

  operator E&() { return static_cast<E
&>(*this); }
  operator E const&() const { return
static_cast<const E&>(*this); }
};

// The actual Vec class:
class Vec : public
VecExpression<Vec> {
  std::vector<double> _data;
public:
  typedef std::vector<double>::size
_type size_type;
  typedef std::vector<double>::value
_type value_type;
  typedef
std::vector<double>::reference
reference;

  reference operator[](size_type i) {
return _data[i]; }
  value_type operator[](size_type i)
const { return _data[i]; }
  size_type size() const { return _data.
size(); }

  Vec(size_type n) : _data(n) {} //
Construct a given size:

  // Construct from any VecExpression:
  template <typename E>
  Vec(VecExpression<E> const& vec)
{
    E const& v = vec;
    _data.resize(v.size());
    for (size_type i = 0; i != v.size(); +
+i) {
      _data[i] = v[i];
    }
  }
};

template <typename E1, typename E2>
class VecDifference : public
VecExpression<VecDifference<E1,
E2> > {
  E1 const& _u;
  E2 const& _v;
public:
  typedef Vec::size_type size_type;
  typedef Vec::value_type value_type;
  VecDifference(VecExpression<E1>
const& u, VecExpression<E2> const&
v) : _u(u), _v(v) {
    assert(u.template size<E1>() == v.
template size<E2>());
  }
  size_type size() const { return _v.
size(); }
  value_type operator[](Vec::size_type
i) const { return _u[i] - _v[i]; }
};

template <typename E>
class VecScaled : public
VecExpression<VecScaled<E> > {
  double _alpha;
  E const& _v;
public:
  VecScaled(double alpha,
VecExpression<E> const& v) :
_alpha(alpha), _v(v) {}
  Vec::size_type size() const { return
_v.size(); }
  Vec::value_type operator[](Vec::size
_type i) const { return _alpha * _v[i]; }
};


// Now we can overload operators:

template <typename E1, typename E2>
VecDifference<E1,E2> const
operator-(VecExpression<E1> const&
u, VecExpression<E2> const& v) {
  return VecDifference<E1,E2>(u,v);
}

template <typename E>
VecScaled<E> const
operator*(double alpha,
VecExpression<E> const& v) {
  return VecScaled<E>(alpha,v);
}
```

With the above definitions, the expression alpha*(u-v) is of type

```
VecScaled<VecDifference<Vec,Vec>
>
```

so calling Vec x = alpha * (u-v) calls the constructor that takes a VecExpression<VecScaled<VecDiffere > >. Each line of the for loop then expands from

```
_data[i] = v[i];
```

to essentially

```
_data[i] = alpha * (u[i] - v[i]);
```

with no temporaries needed and only one pass through each memory block. Source (edited): "http://en.wikipedia.org/wiki/Expression_templates"

fstream

fstream is a standard C++ library that handles reading from and writing to files either in text or in binary formats. It is an object oriented alternative to C's FILE from the C standard library.

ofstream

fstream can both input and output to files in several modes. The following example creates a file called 'file.txt' and puts the text 'Hello World' followed by a newline into it.

```
#include <fstream>

int main()
{
   std::ofstream file;// can be merged
to std::ofstream file("file.txt");
   file.open("file.txt");
   file << "Hello world!\n";
   file.close();// is not necessary
because the destructor closes the open
file by default
   return 0;
}
```

ifstream

ifstream is the C++ standard library class that provides an interface to read data from files as input streams. The input stream may open a file in the constructor, just like an output stream. ifstream inf("input.dat", ifstream::in); //ifstream::in is a default, so it could be omitted

or afterwards:

ifstream inf; inf.open("input.dat");

To close a stream, one uses the close method: inf.close();

The ifstream destructor will close the file cleanly as well. It is perfectly acceptable to allow the ifstream object to fall out of scope without calling close. This is often a desirable style, as it simplifies the "clean up" process when an exception is thrown or an error is otherwise encountered.

This would be a basic cat utility:

```
#include <iostream>
#include <fstream>
#include <string>

using std::cin;
using std::cout;
using std::cerr;

void print(std::istream& in)
{
        try{
                std::string tmp;
                while(1){
                        std::getline(in,tmp);
                        tmp+='\n';
                        cout.write(tmp.c
_str(),tmp.length());
                }
        }
        catch(std::ifstream::failure
e){
                if(!in.eof())
                        cerr << e.what()
<<'\n';
        }

}

int main(int argc,char** argv)
{

    std::ifstream in;
    in.exceptions(
std::ifstream::eofbit |
std::ifstream::failbit |
std::ifstream::badbit );
    cin.exceptions(
std::ifstream::eofbit |
std::ifstream::failbit |
std::ifstream::badbit );

    if(argc==1){
        print(cin);
    }
    try{
        for(int i=1;i<argc;i++){

            if(argv[i]==std::string("-
")){
                print(cin);
            }
            else{
                in.open(argv[i]);
                print(in);
            }
        }
    }
    catch(std::ifstream::failure e){
        cerr << e.what();
    }

}
```

Source (edited): "http://en.wikipedia.org/wiki/Fstream"

Functional (C++)

A **Function Object**, or **Functor**, in C++ is simply any object that can be called as if it is a function. A Function Object could be an ordinary function or a function pointer. More generally, it could be an object of a class that defines operator.

No STL algorithms require function objects of more than two arguments. Function objects that return bool are an important special case. A Unary function whose return type is bool is called a Predicate, and a Binary Function whose return type is bool is called a Binary Predicate.

Adaptable function objects

In general, a function object has restrictions on the type of its argument. The type restrictions need not be simple, though: operator() may be overloaded, or may be a member template, or both. Similarly, there need be no way for a program to determine what those restrictions are. An adaptable function object, however, does specify what the argument and return types are, and provides nested typedefs so that those types can be named and used in programs. If a type F0 is a model of Adaptable Generator, then it must define F0::result_type. Similarly, if F1 is a model of Adaptable Unary Function then it must define F1::argument_type and F1::result_type, and if F2 is a model of Adaptable Binary Function then it must define F2::first_argument_type, F2::second_argument_type, and F2::result_type. The STL provides base classes unary_function and binary_function to simplify the definition of Adaptable Unary Functions and Adaptable Binary Functions.

Adaptable function objects are important because they can be used by function object adaptors: function objects that transform or manipulate other function objects. The STL provides many different function object adaptors, including unary_negate (which returns the logical complement of the value returned by a particular Adaptable Predicate), and unary_compose and binary_compose, which perform composition of function object.

Predefined function objects

The STL includes many different predefined function objects, including arithmetic operations (plus, minus, multiplies, divides, modulus, and negate), comparisons (equal_to, not_equal_to greater, less, greater_equal, and less_equal), and logical operations (logical_and, logical_or, and logical_not). It is possible to perform very sophisticated operations without actually writing a new function object, simply by combining predefined function objects and function object adaptors.

Source (edited): "http://en.wikipedia.org/wiki/Functional_(C%2B%2B)"

GNU E

GNU E is an extension of C++ designed for writing software systems to support persistent applications, it was designed as part of the Exodus project.

Source (edited): "http://en.wikipedia.org/wiki/GNU_E"

Header-only

In the context of the C or C++ programming languages, a library is called **header-only** if the full definitions of all macros, functions and classes comprising the library are visible to the compiler in a header file form. Header-only libraries do not need to be separately compiled, packaged and installed in order to be used. All that is required is to point the compiler at the location of the headers (the -I switch in gcc/g++), and then #include the header files into the application source.

The disadvantages include:

- brittleness – most changes to the library will require recompilation of all compilation units using that library
- longer compilation times – the compilation unit must see the implementation of all components in the included files, rather than just their interfaces
- code-bloat (this may be disputed) – the necessary use of inline statements in non-class functions can lead to code bloat by over-inlining.

Nonetheless, the header-only form is popular because it avoids the (often much more serious) problem of packaging.

List of (mostly) header-only libraries

- Some of the Boost C++ Libraries
- STLSoft C++ Libraries
- VOLE
- flecxx
- STL

Source (edited): "http://en.wikipedia.org/wiki/Header-only"

Header file

Some programming languages (most notably C, C++, and Objective-C) use **header files**. These files allow programmers to separate certain elements of a program's source code into reusable files. Header files commonly contain forward declarations of classes, subroutines, variables, and other identifiers. Programmers who wish to declare standardized identifiers in more than one source file can place such identifiers in a single header file, which other code can then include whenever the header contents are required. This is to keep the interface in the header separate from the implementation. The C standard library and C++ standard library traditionally declare their standard functions in header files.

Newer compiled languages (such as Java, C#) do not use forward declarations; identifiers are recognized automatically from source files and read directly from dynamic library symbols. This means header files are not needed.

Motivation

In most modern computer programming languages, programmers can break up programs into smaller components (such as classes and subroutines) and distribute those components among many translation units (typically in the form of physical source files), which the system can compile separately. Once a subroutine needs to be used somewhere other than in the translation unit where it is defined, a way to refer to it must exist. For example, a function defined in this way in one source file:

```
int add(int a, int b)
{
    return a + b;
}
```

may be declared (with a function prototype) and then referred to in a second source file as follows:

```
int add(int, int);

int triple(int x)
{
    return add(x, add(x, x));
}
```

One drawback of this method is that the prototype must be present in all files that use the function. Another drawback is that if the return type or arguments of the function are changed, these prototypes will have to be updated. This process can be automated with the C preprocessor (i.e., getting *any* prototype results in getting the *latest* one). For example, the following code declares the function in a separate file (the parameter names are not used by the compiler, but they can be useful to programmers):
File "add.h"

```
#ifndef ADD_H_GUARD
#define ADD_H_GUARD
int add(int a, int b);
#endif
```

This file uses include guards to avoid multiple definitions of the function. The following code demonstrates how header files are used:

```
#include "add.h"
int triple(int x,int y)
{
    return add(x,add(x,x));
}
```

Now, every time the code is compiled, the latest function prototypes in add.h will be included in the files using them, avoiding potentially disastrous errors.

Alternatives

Some newer languages (such as Java) dispense with header files and instead use a naming scheme that allows the compiler to locate the source files associated with interfaces and class implementations. These languages (and perhaps others) preserve type information for functions in the object code, allowing the linker to verify that functions are used correctly.

COBOL and RPG IV have a form of include files called *copybooks*. Programmers "include" these into the source of the program in a similar way to header files, but they also allow replacing certain text in them with other text. The COBOL keyword for inclusion is COPY, and replacement is done with a REPLACING ... BY ... clause.

Fortran does not require header files per se. However, Fortran 90 and later has two related features: include statements and modules. The former can be used to share a common file containing procedure interfaces, much like a C header, although the specification of an interface is not required for all varieties of Fortran procedures. This approach is not commonly used; instead procedures are generally grouped into modules which can then be referenced with a use statement within other regions of code. For modules, header-type interface information is automatically generated by the compiler, and typically put into separate module (usually *.mod) files in a compiler-dependent format, although some compilers have placed this information directly into object files. Note that the language specification itself does not mandate the creation of any extra files, even though module procedure interfaces are almost universally propagated in this manner.
Source (edited): "http://en.wikipedia.org/wiki/Header_file"

Herb Sutter

Herb Sutter 2009

Herb Sutter is a prominent C++ expert. He is also a book author and a columnist for Dr. Dobb's Journal. He joined Microsoft in 2002 as a platform evangelist for Visual C++ .NET, rising to lead software architect for C++/CLI. Sutter served as secretary and convener of the ISO C++ standards committee for over 10 years. In September 2008 he was replaced by P.J. Plauger.

Guru of the Week

From 1997 to 2003, Sutter regularly created C++ programming problems and posted them on the Usenet newsgroup comp.lang.c++.moderated, under the title *Guru of the Week*. The problems generally addressed common misconceptions or poorly understood concepts in C++. Sutter later published expanded versions of many of the problems in his first two books, *Exceptional C++* and *More Exceptional C++*.

Source (edited): "http://en.wikipedia.org/wiki/Herb_Sutter"

ifstream

ifstream is the C++ standard library class that provides an interface to read data from files as input streams.

To use the **ifstream** class, fstream library (header file) must be included using the preprocessor directive: #include <fstream>

The input stream may open a file in the constructor:

ifstream inf("input.dat", ifstream::in);

or afterwards:

ifstream inf; inf.open("input.dat");

To close a stream, one uses the close method: inf.close();

The ifstream destructor will close the file cleanly as well. It is perfectly acceptable to allow the ifstream object to fall out of scope without calling close. This is often a desirable style, as it simplifies the "clean up" process when an exception is thrown or an error is otherwise encountered.

Source (edited): "http://en.wikipedia.org/wiki/Ifstream"

Inner class

In object-oriented programming (OOP), an **inner class** or **nested class** is a class declared entirely within the body of another class or interface. It is distinguished from a subclass.

Overview

An instance of a normal or top-level class can exist on its own. By contrast, an instance of an inner class cannot be instantiated without being bound to a top-level class.

Let us take the abstract notion of a Car with four Wheels. Our Wheels have a specific feature that relies on being part of our Car. This notion does not represent the Wheels as Wheels in a more general form that could be part of a vehicle. Instead, it represents them as specific to this one. We can model this notion using inner classes as follows:

We have the top-level class Car. Instances of Class Car are composed of four instances of the class Wheel. This particular implementation of Wheel is specific to the car, so the code does not model the general notion of a wheel that would be better represented as a top-level class. Therefore, it is semantically connected to the class Car and the code of Wheel is in some way coupled to its outer class.

Inner classes provide us with a mechanism to accurately model this connection. We say that our Wheel class is Car. Wheel, Car being the top-level class and Wheel being the inner class.

Inner classes therefore allow for the object orientation of certain parts of the program that would otherwise not be encapsulated into a class.

Larger segments of code within a class might be better modeled or refactored as a separate top-level class, rather than an inner class. This would make the code more general in its application and therefore more re-usable but potentially might be premature generalization. This may prove more effective, if code has many inner classes with the shared functionality.

Types of inner classes

In Java there are four types of **nested** class:

Static

- Static member class, also called *static nested classes* - They are declared static. Like other things in static scope (i.e. static methods), they do not have an enclosing instance, and cannot access instance variables and methods of the enclosing class. They are almost identical to non-nested classes except for scope details (they can refer to static variables and methods of the enclosing class without qualifying the name; other classes that are not one of its enclosing classes have to qualify its name with its enclosing class's name). Nested interfaces are implicitly static.

Non-Static / Inner Classes

Inner class - The following categories are called *inner classes*. Each instance of these classes has a reference to an *enclosing instance* (i.e. an instance of the enclosing class), except for local and anonymous classes declared in static context. Hence, they can implicitly refer to instance variables and methods of the enclosing class. The enclosing instance reference can be explicitly obtained via EnclosingClassName.this. Inner classes may not have static variables or methods, except for compile-time constant variables. When they are created, they must have a reference to an instance of the enclosing class; which means they must either be created within an instance method or constructor of the enclosing class, or (for member and anonymous classes) be created using the syntax enclosingInstance.new InnerClass().

- Member class - They are declared outside a function (hence a "member") and not declared "static".
- Local class - These are classes that are declared in the body of a function. They can only be referred to in the rest of the function. They can use local variables and parameters of the function, but only ones that are declared "final". (This is because the local class instance must maintain a separate copy of the variable, as it may out-live the function; so as not to have the confusion of two modifiable variables with the same name in the same scope, the variable is forced to be non-modifiable.)
- Anonymous class - These are local classes that are automatically declared and instantiated in the middle of an expression. They can only directly extend one class or implement one interface. They can specify arguments to the constructor of the superclass, but cannot otherwise have a constructor (however, this is not a limitation, since it can have an instance initializer block to perform any initialization).

Programming Languages

- Inner classes became a feature of the Java programming language starting with version 1.1.
- They are also a feature of the D programming language, Visual Basic . NET, C++ and C#.
- In Python, it is possible to nest a class within another class, method or function.
- C++ has nested classes that are like Java's static member classes, except that they are not declared with "static".

GUI code

Local inner classes are often used in Java to define callbacks for GUI code. Components can then share an object that implements an event handling interface or extends an abstract adapter class, containing the code to be executed when a given event is triggered.

Anonymous inner classes are also used where the event handling code is only used by one component and therefore does not need a named reference.

This avoids a large monolithic **actionPerformed(ActionEvent)** method with multiple if-else branches to identify the source of the event. This type of code is often considered messy and the inner class variations are considered to be better in all regards.

Source (edited): "http://en.wikipedia.org/wiki/Inner_class"

ios (C++)

ios is a header file in the C++ standard library which defines several types and functions basic to the operation of iostreams. This header is typically included automatically by other iostream headers. Programmers rarely include it directly.

Source (edited): "http://en.wikipedia.org/wiki/Ios_(C%2B%2B)"

List of C++ multi-threading libraries

List of cross-platform multi-threading libraries for the c++ programming language.

- Rogue Wave Libraries
- Boost C++ Libraries
- Intel Threading Building Blocks
- OpenMP
- OpenThreads
- POCO Thread (part of POCO project -)
- POSIX Threads
- tinythread++
- Zthread

Source (edited): "http://en.wikipedia.org/wiki/List_of_C%2B%2B_multi-threading_libraries"

List of C++ template libraries

The following **list of C++ template libraries** details the various libraries of templates available for the C++ programming language.

General

- Standard Template Library
- Boost C++ Libraries

- ODB ORM and Database-Aware Container Template Library
- STLSoft C++ Libraries
- Electronic Arts Standard Template Library
- Adobe Source Libraries
- Intel Threading Building Blocks
- C++ Templated Image Processing Library
- Database Template Library
- Oracle Template Library
- Windows Template Library
- Armadillo C++ Library (linear algebra)
- Dlib C++ Library
- Eigen Library (linear algebra)
- Matrix Template Library
- Loki (C++)
- Native Template Library
- PoCo C++ Libraries
- CGAL
- Blitz++
- Adaptive Communication Environment
- View Template Library
- STXXL : Standard Template Library for Extra Large Data Sets
- STLPort

Source (edited): "http://en.wikipedia.org/wiki/List_of_C%2B%2B_template_libraries"

Loki (C++)

Loki is the name of a C++ software library written by Andrei Alexandrescu as part of his book Modern C++ Design.

The library makes extensive use of C++ template metaprogramming and implements several commonly used tools: typelist, functor, singleton, smart pointer, object factory, visitor and multimethods.

Originally the library was only compatible with two of the most standard conforming C++ compilers (CodeWarrior and Comeau C/C++): later efforts have made it usable with a wide array of compilers (including older Visual C ++ 6.0, Borland C++ Builder 6.0, and GCC). Compiler vendors used Loki as a compatibility benchmark, further increasing the number of compliant compilers.

Maintenance and further development of Loki has been continued through an open-source community led by Peter Kümmel and Richard Sposato as a Sourceforge project. Ongoing contributions by many people have improved the overall robustness and functionality of the library. Loki is not tied to the book anymore as it already has a lot of new components (e.g. - StrongPtr, Printf, and Scopeguard). Loki inspired similar tools and functionality now also present in the Boost library collection.

Source (edited): "http://en.wikipedia.org/wiki/Loki_(C%2B%2B)"

Mentat (computing)

Mentat is the name given to a macro-dataflow extension of the C++ programming language. It was developed at the University of Virginia computer science Department by a research group led by Andrew Grimshaw. The combination of the ideas needed to implement the Mentat run-time with the ideas in Carnegie Mellon University's Hydra distributed operating system led to the Legion distributed OS.

Source (edited): "http://en.wikipedia.org/wiki/Mentat_(computing)"

Microsoft Visual C++ Name Mangling

Microsoft Visual C++ Name Mangling is a mangling (decoration) scheme used in Microsoft Visual C++ series of compilers. It provides a way of encoding name and additional information about a function, structure, class or another datatype in order to pass more semantic information from the Microsoft Visual C++ compiler to its linker.

Overview

The C++ language does not define a standard decoration scheme, so Microsoft Visual C++ uses its own.

Any object code produced by the compiler is usually linked with other pieces of object code by the linker. The linker relies on unique object names for identification but C++ (and many modern programming languages) allows different entities to be named with the same identifier as long as they occupy a different namespace. So names should be mangled by the compiler to make them distinct before reaching the linker. The linker also needs a great deal of information on each program entity. For example, to correctly link a function it needs its name, the number of arguments and their types, and so on.

C++ decoration can become fairly complex (storing information about classes, templates, namespaces, operator overloading, etc.). This section explains the specific manner in which the Microsoft Visual C++ series of compilers mangle symbol names.

Basic Structure

All mangled C++ names start with ? (question mark). Because all mangled C names start with alphanumeric characters, @ (at-sign) and _ (underscore), C++ names can be distinguished from C names.

The structure of mangled names looks like this:

- Prefix ?

- *Optional*: Prefix @?
- Qualified name
- Type information (see below)

Function

Type information in function names generally looks like this:

- Access level and function type
- *Conditional*: CV-class modifier of function, if non-static member function
- Function property

Data

Type information in data names looks like this:

- Access level and storage class
- Data type
- CV-class modifier

Elements

Mangled name contains a lot of elements which will be discussed.

Name

Qualified name consists of the following fragments:

- Basic name: one of: name fragment or special name
- Qualification #1: one of: name fragment, name with template arguments, numbered namespace or back reference
- Qualification #2
- ...
- Terminator @

Qualification is written in reversed order. For example myclass::nested::something becomes something@nested@myclass@@.

Name Fragment

A fragment of a name is simply represented as the name with trailing @.

Special Name

Special names are represented as a code with a preceding ?. Most of special names are constructor, destructor, operator and internal symbol. Below is a table for known codes.
Prefix _P is used as ?_PX, though I don't know about it.

Below are the RTTI-related codes (all starting with _R). Some codes have trailing parameters.

Name with Template Arguments

Name fragments starting with ?$ have template arguments. This kind of name looks like this:

- Prefix ?$
- Name terminated by @
- Template argument list

For example, we assume the following prototype.

```
void __cdecl
abc<def<int>,void*>::xyz(void);
```

The name of this function can be obtained by the following process:

```
abc<def<int>,void*>::xyz
xyz@ abc<def<int>,void*> @
xyz@ ?$abc@ def<int> void* @ @
xyz@ ?$abc@ V def<int> @ PAX @
@
xyz@ ?$abc@ V ?$def@H@ @ PAX
@ @
xyz@?$abc@V?$def@H@@PAX@@
```

So the mangled name for this function is ?xyz@?$abc@V?$def@H@@PAX@@YAXXZ.

Nested Name

A name fragment starting with ?? denotes a nested name. This is a name inside a local scope which must be exported. Its structure looks like the following:

- Prefix ?
- C++ Mangled name (so starting with ? again)

For example, ?nested@??func@@YAXXZ@4HA means variable ?nested@@4HA(int nested) inside ?func@@YAXXZ(void __cdecl func(void)). The UnDecorateSymbolName function returns int 'void __cdecl func(void)'::nested for this input.

Numbered Namespace

In qualification, a numbered namespace is represented as a preceding ? and an unsigned number. The UnDecorateSymbolName function returns something like '42' for this kind of input.

Exceptionally, if a numbered namespace starts with ?A, it becomes an anonymous namespace ('anonymous namespace').
Source (edited): "http://en.wikipedia.org/wiki/Microsoft_Visual_C%2B%2B_Name_Mangling"

Mophun

Mophun, a product of Synergenix Interactive, is an environment for developing Mobile-Phone Games and Applications. The games are developed in the C and C++ programming languages using an open source SDK available upon request from the website. A compiler translates the projects into a system independent application. There are no freeware Mophun applications available because any applications need to be certified before they are allowed to run on a compatible device.

Mophun was the brainchild of Antony Hartley and was developed by Hartley and Anders Norlander. Antony Hartley since moved on to form Mobile Sorcery, a company that specializes in visual mobile authoring.
Source (edited): "http://en.wikipedia.org/wiki/Mophun"

Most vexing parse

The **most vexing parse** is a specific form of syntactic ambiguity resolution in the C++ programming language. The term was used by Scott Meyers in *Effective STL* (2001). It is formally defined in section 6.8 of the C++ language standard.

Example with classes

An example is:

```
class Timer {
 public:
  Timer();
};

class TimeKeeper {
 public:
  TimeKeeper(const Timer& t);

  int get_time();
};

int main() {
  TimeKeeper time_keeper(Timer());
  return time_keeper.get_time();
}
```

The line

```
  TimeKeeper time_keeper(Timer());
```

could be disambiguated either as

- a variable definition for variable time_keeper of class TimeKeeper, taking an anonymous instance of class Timer or
- a function declaration for a function time_keeper which returns an object of type TimeKeeper and takes a single (unnamed) argument which is a function returning type Timer (and taking no input). (See Function object#In C and C++)

Most programmers expect the first, but the C++ standard requires it to be interpreted as the second.

For example, g++ gives the following error message:

```
$ g++ -c time_keeper.cc
time_keeper.cc: In function 'int main()':
time_keeper.cc:15: error: request for member 'get_time' in 'time_keeper', which is
  of non-class type 'TimeKeeper(Timer (*)())'
```

Clang++ provides a useful warning:

```
$ clang++ time_keeper.cc
time_keeper.cc:14:25: warning: parentheses were disambiguated as a function declarator
  TimeKeeper time_keeper(Timer());
                        ~~~~~~~~~
```

One way to force the compiler to consider this as a variable definition is to add an extra pair of parentheses:

```
TimeKeeper time_keeper( (Timer()) );
```

Example with functions

An even simpler example appears when a functional cast is intended to convert an expression for initializing a variable or passing to a constructor parameter

```
void f(double adouble) {
  int i(int(adouble));
}
```

In this case, the parentheses around "adouble" are superfluous and the declaration of "i" is again a function declaration equivalent to the following

```
// takes an integer and returns an integer
int i(int adouble);
```

To disambiguate this in favour of a variable declaration, the same technique can be used as for the first case above. Another solution is to use the cast notation or to use a named cast

```
// declares a variable called 'i'
int i(static_cast<int>(adouble));
```

Source (edited): "http://en.wikipedia.org/wiki/Most_vexing_parse"

Name mangling

In software compiler engineering, **name mangling** (also called **name decoration**) is a technique used to solve various problems caused by the need to resolve unique names for programming entities in many modern programming languages.

It provides a way of encoding additional information in the name of a function, structure, class or another datatype in order to pass more semantic information from the compilers to linkers.

The need arises where the language allows different entities to be named with the same identifier as long as they occupy a different namespace (where a namespace is typically defined by a module, class, or explicit *namespace* directive).

Any object code produced by compilers is usually linked with other pieces of object code (produced by the same or another compiler) by a type of program called a linker. The linker needs a great deal of information on each program entity. For example, to correctly link a function it needs its name, the number of arguments and their types, and so on.

C name decoration in Microsoft Windows

Although name mangling is not generally required or used by languages that do not support function overloading (such as C and classic Pascal), they use it in some cases to provide additional information about a function. For example, compilers targeted at Microsoft Windows platforms support a variety of calling conventions, which determine the manner in which parameters are sent to subroutines and results returned. Because the different calling conventions are not compatible with one another, compilers mangle symbols with codes detailing which convention should be used.

The mangling scheme was established by Microsoft, and has been informally followed by other compilers including Digital Mars, Borland, and GNU gcc, when compiling code for the Windows platforms. The scheme even applies to other languages, such as Pascal, D, Delphi, Fortran, and C#. This allows subroutines written in those languages to call, or be called by, existing Windows libraries using a calling convention different from their default.

When compiling the following C examples:

```
int _cdecl    f (int x) { return 0; }
int _stdcall  g (int y) { return 0; }
int _fastcall h (int z) { return 0; }
```

32 bit compilers emit, respectively:

```
_f
_g@4
@h@4
```

In the stdcall and fastcall mangling schemes, the function is encoded as **_name@X** and **@name@X** respectively, where **X** is the number of bytes, in decimal, of the argument(s) in the parameter list (including those passed in registers, for fastcall). In the case of cdecl, the function name is merely prefixed by an underscore.

Note that the 64-bit convention on Windows (Microsoft C) is no leading underscore. This difference may in some rare cases lead to unresolved externals when porting such code to 64 bits. For example, Fortran code can use 'alias' to link against a C method by name as follows:

```
SUBROUTINE f()
!DEC$ ATTRIBUTES C, ALIAS:'_f'
:: f
END SUBROUTINE
```

This will compile and link fine under 32 bits, but generate an unresolved external '_f' under 64 bits. One work around for this is to not use 'alias' at all (in which the method names typically need to be capitalized in C and Fortran), or to use the BIND option:

```
SUBROUTINE f() BIND(C,NAME
="f")
END SUBROUTINE
```

Name mangling in C++

C++ compilers are the most widespread and yet least standard users of name mangling. The first C++ compilers were implemented as translators to C source code, which would then be compiled by a C compiler to object code; because of this, symbol names had to conform to C identifier rules. Even later, with the emergence of compilers which produced machine code or assembly directly, the system's linker generally did not support C++ symbols, and mangling was still required.

The C++ language does not define a standard decoration scheme, so each compiler uses its own. C++ also has complex language features, such as classes, templates, namespaces, and operator overloading, that alter the meaning of specific symbols based on context or usage. Meta-data about these features can be disambiguated by mangling (decorating) the name of a symbol. Because the name-mangling systems for such features are not standardized across compilers, few linkers can link object code that was produced by different compilers.

Simple example

Consider the following two definitions of f() in a C++ program:

```
int  f (void) { return 1; }
int  f (int)  { return 0; }
void g (void) { int i = f(), j = f(0); }
```

These are distinct functions, with no relation to each other apart from the name. If they were natively translated into C with no changes, the result would be an error — C does not permit two functions with the same name. The C++ compiler therefore will encode the type information in the symbol name, the result being something resembling:

```
int  __f_v (void) { return 1; }
int  __f_i (int)  { return 0; }
void __g_v (void) { int i = __f_v(), j =
__f_i(0); }
```

Notice that g() is mangled even though there is no conflict; name mangling applies to **all** symbols.

Complex example

For a more complex example, we'll consider an example of a real-world name mangling implementation: that used by GNU GCC 3.*x*, and how it mangles the following example class. The mangled symbol is shown below the respective identifier name.

```
namespace wikipedia
{
  class article
  {
  public:
    std::string format (void);
      /* =
_ZN9wikipedia7article6formatEv */

    bool print_to (std::ostream&);
      /* = _ZN9wikipedia7article8print
_toERSo */

    class wikilink
    {
    public:
      wikilink (std::string const&
name);
        /* =
_ZN9wikipedia7article8wikilinkC1ERK
*/
    };
  };
}
```

All mangled symbols begin with **_Z** (note that an underscore followed by a capital is a reserved identifier in C and C++, so conflict with user identifiers is avoided); for nested names (including both namespaces and classes), this is followed by **N**, then a series of <length, id> pairs (the length being the length of the next identifier), and finally **E**. For example, wikipedia::article::format becomes

_ZN·*9***wikipedia**·*7***article**·*6***format**·E

For functions, this is then followed by the type information; as format() is a void function, this is simply **v**; hence:

_ZN·9**wikipedia**·7**article**·6**format**·E·v

For print_to, a standard type std::ostream (or more properly std::basic_ostream<char, char_traits<char> >) is used, which has the special alias **So**; a reference to this type is therefore **RSo**, with the complete name for the function being:

_ZN·9**wikipedia**·7**article**·8**print_to**·E·**RSo**

How different compilers mangle the same functions

There isn't a standard scheme by which even trivial C++ identifiers are mangled, and consequently different compiler vendors (or even different versions of the same compiler, or the same compiler on different platforms) mangle public symbols in radically different (and thus totally incompatible) ways. Consider how different C++ compilers mangle the same functions:

Notes:

- The Compaq C++ compiler on OpenVMS VAX and Alpha (but not IA-64) and Tru64 has two name mangling schemes. The original, pre-standard scheme is known as ARM model, and is based on the name mangling described in the C++ Annotated Reference Manual (ARM). With the advent of new features in standard C++, particularly templates, the ARM scheme became more and more unsuitable — it could not encode certain function types, or produced identical mangled names for different functions. It was therefore replaced by the newer "ANSI" model, which supported all ANSI template features, but was not backwards compatible.
- On IA-64, a standard ABI exists (see external links), which defines (among other things) a standard name-mangling scheme, and which is used by all the IA-64 compilers. GNU GCC 3.*x*, in addition, has adopted the name mangling scheme defined in this standard for use on other, non-Intel platforms.

Handling of C symbols when linking from C++

The job of the common C++ idiom:

```
#ifdef __cplusplus
extern "C" {
#endif
  /* ... */
#ifdef __cplusplus
}
#endif
```

is to ensure that the symbols following are "unmangled" – that the compiler emits a binary file with their names undecorated, as a C compiler would do. As C language definitions are unmangled, the C++ compiler needs to avoid mangling references to these identifiers.

For example, the standard strings library, <string.h> usually contains something resembling:

```
#ifdef __cplusplus
extern "C" {
#endif

void *memset (void *, int, size_t);
char *strcat (char *, const char *);
int  strcmp (const char *, const char *);
char *strcpy (char *, const char *);

#ifdef __cplusplus
}
#endif
```

Thus, code such as:

```
if (strcmp(argv[1], "-x") == 0)
  strcpy(a, argv[2]);
else
  memset (a, 0, sizeof(a));
```

uses the correct, unmangled strcmp and memset. If the extern had not been used, the (SunPro) C++ compiler would produce code equivalent to:

```
if (__1cGstrcmp6Fpkc1_i_(argv[1], "-x") == 0)
  __1cGstrcpy6Fpcpkc_0_(a, argv[2]);
else
  __1cGmemset6FpviI_0_ (a, 0, sizeof(a));
```

Since those symbols do not exist in the C runtime library (*e.g.* libc), link errors would result.

Standardised name mangling in C++

While it is a relatively common belief that standardised name mangling in the C++ language would lead to greater interoperability between implementations, this is not really the case. Name mangling is only one of several application binary interface issues in a C++ implementation. Other ABI issues like exception handling, virtual table layout, structure padding, *etc.* cause differing C++ implementations to be incompatible. Further, requiring a particular form of mangling would cause issues for systems where implementation limits (*e.g.* length of symbols) dictate a particular mangling scheme. A standardised *requirement* for name mangling would also prevent an implementation where mangling was not required at all — for example, a linker which understood the C++ language.

The C++ standard therefore does not attempt to standardise name mangling. On the contrary, the *Annotated C++ Reference Manual* (also known as *ARM*, ISBN 0-201-51459-1, section 7.2.1c) actively encourages the use of different mangling schemes to prevent linking when other aspects of the ABI, such as exception handling and virtual table layout, are incompatible.

Real-world effects of C++ name mangling

Because C++ symbols are routinely exported from DLL and shared object files, the name mangling scheme is not merely a compiler-internal matter. Different compilers (or different versions of the same compiler, in many cases) produce such binaries under different name decoration schemes, meaning that symbols are frequently unresolved if the compilers used to create the library and the program using it employed different schemes. For example, if a system with multiple C++ compilers installed (*e.g.* GNU GCC and the OS vendor's compiler) wished to install the Boost C++ Libraries, it would have to be compiled twice — once for the vendor compiler and once for GCC.

It is good for safety purposes that compilers producing incompatible object codes (codes based on different ABIs, regarding e.g. classes and exceptions) use different name mangling schemes. This guarantees that these incompatibilities are detected at the linking phase, not when executing the software (which could lead to obscure bugs and serious stability issues).

For this reason name decoration is an important aspect of any C++-related ABI.

Name mangling in Java

The language, compiler, and .class file format were all designed together (and had object-orientation in mind from the start), so the primary problem solved by name mangling doesn't exist in implementations of the Java runtime. There are, however, cases where an analogous transformation and qualification of names is necessary.

Creating unique names for inner and anonymous classes

The scope of anonymous classes is confined to their parent class, so the compiler must produce a "qualified" public name for the inner class, to avoid conflict where other classes (inner or not) exist in the same namespace. Similarly, anonymous classes must have "fake" public names generated for them (as the concept of anonymous classes exists only in the compiler, not the runtime). So, compiling the following java program

```
public class foo {
  class bar {
    public int x;
  }

  public void zark () {
    Object f = new Object () {
      public String toString() {
        return "hello";
      }
    };
  }
}
```

will produce three **.class** files:

- **foo.class**, containing the main (outer) class *foo*
- **foo$bar.class**, containing the named inner class *foo.bar*
- **foo$1.class**, containing the anonymous inner class (local to method *foo.zark*)

All of these class names are valid (as $ symbols are permitted in the JVM specification) and these names are "safe" for the compiler to generate, as the Java language definition prohibits $ symbols in normal java class definitions.

Name resolution in Java is further complicated at runtime, as fully qualified class names are unique only inside a specific classloader instance. Classloaders are ordered hierarchically and each Thread in the JVM has a so called context class loader, so in cases where two different classloader instances contain classes with the same name, the system first tries to load the class using the root (or system) classloader and then goes down the hierarchy to the context class loader.

Java Native Interface

Java's native method support allows java language programs to call out to programs written in another language (generally either C or C++). There are two name-resolution concerns here, neither of which is implemented in a particularly standard manner:

- Java to native name translation
- normal C++ name mangling

Name mangling in Python

A Python programmer can explicitly designate that the name of an attribute within a class body should be mangled by using a name with two leading underscores and not more than one trailing underscore. For example, __thing will be mangled, as will ___thing and __thing_, but __thing__ and __thing___ will not. On encountering these, Python transforms these names by a single underscore and the name of the enclosing class.

So, for example,

```
class Test(object):
  def __mangled_name(self):
    pass
  def normal_name(self):
    pass

print dir(Test)
```

will output:

```
['_Test__mangled_name',
'__doc__',
'__module__',
'normal_name']
```

Name mangling in Borland's Turbo Pascal / Delphi range

To avoid name mangling in Pascal, use:

```
exports
  myFunc name 'myFunc', myProc
name 'myProc';
```

Name mangling in Objective-C

Essentially two forms of method exist in Objective-C, the class ("static") method, and the instance method. A method declaration in Objective-C is of the following form

+ *method name*: *argument name*:*parameter* ...
- *method name*: *argument name*:*parameter* ...

Class methods are signified by +, instance methods use -. A typical class method declaration may then look like:

```
+ (id) initWithX: (int) number andY:
(int) number;
+ (id) new;
```

with instance methods looking like

- (id) value;
- (id) setValue: (id) new_value;

Each of these method declarations have a specific internal representation. When compiled, each method is named according to the following scheme for class methods:

_c_*Class_methodname_name_name_* ...

and this for instance methods:

_i_*Class_methodname_name_name_* ...

The colons in the Objective-C syntax are translated to underscores. So, the Objective-C class method + (id) initWithX: (int) number andY: (int) number;, if belonging to the Point class would translate as _c_Point_initWithX_andY_, and the instance method (belonging to the same class) - (id) value; would translate to _i_Point_value.

Each of the methods of a class are labeled in this way. However, in order to look up a method that a class may respond to would be tedious if all methods are represented in this fashion. Each of the methods is assigned a unique symbol (such as an integer). Such a symbol is known as a *selector*. In Objective-C, one can manage selectors directly — they have a specific type in Objective-C — SEL.

During compilation, a table is built that maps the textual representation (such as _i_Point_value) to selectors (which are given a type SEL). Managing selectors is more efficient than manipulating the textual representation of a method. Note that a selector only matches a method's name, not the class it belongs to — different classes can have different implementations of a method with the same name. Because of this, implementations of a method are given a specific identifier too — these are known as implementation pointers, and are given a type also, IMP.

Message sends are encoded by the compiler as calls to the id objc_msgSend (id receiver, SEL selector, ...) function, or one of its cousins, where receiver is the receiver of the message, and SEL determines the method to call. Each class has its own table that maps selectors to their implementations — the implementation pointer specifies where in memory the actual implementation of the method resides. There are separate tables for class and instance methods. Apart from being stored in the SEL to IMP lookup tables, the functions are essentially anonymous.

The SEL value for a selector does not vary between classes. This enables polymorphism.

The Objective-C runtime maintains information about the argument and return types of methods. However, this information is not part of the name of the method, and can vary from class to class.

Since Objective-C does not support namespaces, there is no need for mangling of class names (that do appear as symbols in generated binaries).

Name mangling in Fortran

Name mangling is also necessary in Fortran compilers, originally because the language is case insensitive. Further mangling requirements were imposed later in the evolution of the language because of the addition of modules and other features in the Fortran 90 standard. The case mangling, especially, is a common issue that must be dealt with in order to call Fortran libraries (such as LAPACK) from other languages (such as C).

Because of the case insensitivity, the name of a subroutine or function "FOO" must be converted to a canonical case and format by the Fortran compiler so that it will be linked in the same way regardless of case. Different compilers have implemented this in various ways, and no standardization has occurred. The AIX and HP-UX Fortran compilers convert all identifiers to lower case ("foo"), while the Cray Unicos Fortran compilers converted identifiers all upper case ("FOO"). The GNU g77 compiler converts identifiers to lower case plus an underscore ("foo_"), except that identifiers already containing an underscore ("FOO_BAR") have two underscores appended ("foo_bar__"), following a convention established by f2c. Many other compilers, including SGI's IRIX compilers, gfortran, and Intel's Fortran compiler, convert all identifiers to lower case plus an underscore ("foo_" and "foo_bar_").

Identifiers in Fortran 90 modules must be further mangled, because the same subroutine name may apply to different routines in different modules.

Source (edited): "http://en.wikipedia.org/wiki/Name_mangling"

new (C++)

In the C++ programming language, as well as in many C++-based languages, **new** is a language construct that dynamically allocates memory on the heap and initialises the memory using the constructor. Except for a form called the "placement new", new attempts to allocate enough memory on the heap for the new data. If successful, it initialises the memory and returns the address to the newly allocated and initialised memory. However if new cannot allocate memory on the heap it will throw an exception of type std::bad_alloc. This removes the need to explicitly check the result of an allocation.

Syntax

The syntax for new is:

p_var = new typename;

where p_var is a previously declared pointer of type typename. typename can be any basic data type or user-defined object (enum, class, and struct included). If typename is of class type, the default constructor is called to construct the object.

To initialize a new variable created via new, use the following syntax:

```
p_var = new type(initializer);
```

where initializer is the initial value assigned to the new variable, or if type is of class type, initializer is the argument(s) to a constructor.

new can also create an array:

```
p_var = new type [size];
```

In this case, size specifies the length of one-dimensional array to create. The address of the first element is returned and stored into p_var, so

```
p_var[n-1]
```

gives the value of the nth element (counting from 0)

Memory allocated with new must be deallocated with delete to avoid a memory leak. Arrays allocated with new[] must be deallocated with delete[].

```
int *p_scalar = new int(5); //allocates
an integer, set to 5. (same syntax as
constructors)
int *p_array = new int[5]; //allocates
an array of 5 adjacent integers.
(undefined values)
```

Initializers cannot be specified for arrays created with new. All elements of an array are initialized with the default constructor of the type. If the type does not have a default constructor, this is a compile-time error.

Implementation

In compilers conforming to the ISO C++ standard, if there is not enough memory for the allocation, the code throws an exception of type std::bad_alloc. All subsequent code is aborted until the error is handled in a try-catch block or the program exits abnormally. The program does not need to check the value of the pointer; if no exception was thrown, the allocation succeeded. The implemented operations are defined in the header <new>. In most C++ implementations the new operator can also be overloaded to define specific behaviors.

Releasing dynamically allocated memory

Any memory dynamically allocated with new must be released with a delete command. There are two variants: one for arrays and one for single objects.

```
int *p_var = new int;
delete p_var;

int *p_array = new int[50];
delete[] p_array;
```

Note that the compiler is not required to generate a diagnostic message for using the wrong delete. Furthermore, using the inappropriate deallocator will result in undefined behavior.

Reallocating memory allocated by new[]

In contrast to C's realloc, it is not possible to directly reallocate memory allocated with new[]. To extend or reduce the size of a block, one must allocate a new block of adequate size, copy over the old memory, and delete the old block. The C++ standard library provides a dynamic array that can be extended or reduced in its std::vector template.

void* operator new(size_t size)

The C++ language construct that only allocates memory is called void* operator new(size_t size). It is used by new in the allocation phase. It can be overridden per class to define a class specific memory allocator.

Source (edited): "http://en.wikipedia.org/wiki/New_(C%2B%2B)"

ODB (C++)

ODB is an object-relational mapping (ORM) system for the C++ language. It allows an application developer to persist C++ objects to a relational database without having to deal with tables, columns, or SQL and without manually writing any mapping code. ODB is free software and is dual-licensed under the GPL and a proprietary license.

One notable difference between ODB and other ORM implementations for C++ is its automatic generation of the database mapping code and, optionally, the database schema from the C++ headers that declare the classes. This task is performed by the ODB compiler. The ODB compiler is a real C++ compiler except that instead of producing assembly or machine code, it generates portable C++ which can in turn be compiled by any C++ compiler. The ODB compiler uses the GCC compiler frontend for C++ parsing and is implemented using the new GCC plugin architecture.

The other components of the ODB system include the common runtime library (libodb) and the database-specific runtime libraries (for example, libodb-mysql). The common runtime library defines object-oriented database interfaces that are used by the application developer to perform various database operations on persistent objects. The database-specific runtimes implement these interfaces for concrete database systems and provide support functionality for the generated database mapping code.

ODB is not a framework. There is no common base type that all persistent classes should derive from nor are there any restrictions on the data member types in persistent classes. Existing classes can be made persistent with a few or no modifications. ODB is also flexible in the level of insulation it provides to the application developer. It can either completely hide the relational nature of the underlying database or expose some of the details as required.

Mapping

The mapping of C++ classes to database tables is accomplished through a set of custom #pragma directives that are placed in the C++ header file. They allow the application developer to control various aspects of the mapping such as table and column names, C++ types to SQL types mapping, etc. The following example illustrates a typical persistent class declaration:

```
#pragma db object table("people")
class person
{
  ...

private:
  friend class odb::access;
  person ();

  #pragma db id auto
  unsigned long id_;

  string first_;
  string last_;

  #pragma type("INT UNSIGNED")
  unsigned short age_;
};
```

The ODB-specific pragmas can also be placed outside of the class declaration.

Persistence

ODB provides an object-oriented database API that allows the application developer to perform various operations on persistent objects. The following code fragment illustrates the use of the most common operations:

```
unsigned long joe_id = 1;
person john ("John", "Doe", 31);
person jane ("Jane", "Doe", 29);

transaction t (db.begin ());

// Persist in the database.
//
db.persist (john);
db.persist (jane);

// Load from the database.
//
auto_ptr<person> joe (db.
load<person> (joe_id));

// Update in the database.
//
jane.age (jane.age () + 1);
db.update (jane);

// Delete from the database.
//
db.erase (jane);

t.commit ();
```

ODB Query Language

ODB provides an object-oriented query language, called ODB Query Language, which is integrated into C++ allowing the application developer to write expressive and type-safe queries that look and feel like ordinary C++. For example:

```
transaction t (db.begin ());

result r (db.query<person>
(query::last == "Doe" && query::age
< 30));

for (result::iterator i (r.begin ()); i != r.
end (); ++i)
{
  cout << "Hello, " << i->first () <<
endl;
}

t.commit ();
```

Query parameters can be bound to C++ variables either by value or by reference. If desired, native SQL queries can be executed in which case ODB still provides support for parameter binding. Source (edited): "http://en.wikipedia.org/wiki/ODB_(C%2B%2B)"

ObjectCenter

ObjectCenter is the version of CodeCenter for the C++ language. **ObjectCenter** is an integrated development environment (IDE) offering facilities similar to CodeCenter, plus other features such as class browsing facilities. ObjectCenter was formerly named Saber-C++. CodeCenter and ObjectCenter were created by CenterLine Software (formerly Saber Software), a company located in Cambridge, Massachusetts. CenterLine Software later became CenterLine Systems. It was subsequently acquired by Integrated Computer Solutions of Bedford, Massachusetts. Source (edited): "http://en.wikipedia.org/wiki/ObjectCenter"

One Definition Rule

The **One Definition Rule** (**ODR**) is an important concept in the C++ programming language. It's defined in the ISO C++ Standard(ISO/IEC 14882) 2003, at section 3.2.

Summary

In short the ODR states that:

- In any translation unit, a template, type, function, or object can have no more than one definition. Some of these can have any number of declarations. A definition provides an instance.

- In the entire program, an object or non-inline function cannot have more than one definition; if an object or function is used, it must have exactly one definition. You can declare an object or function that is never used, in which case you don't have to provide a definition. In no event can there be more than one definition.
- Some things, like types, templates, and extern inline functions, can be defined in more than one translation unit. For a given entity, each definition must be the same. Non-extern objects and functions in different translation units are different entities, even if their names and types are the same.

Some violations of the ODR must be diagnosed by the compiler. Other violations, particularly those that span translation units, are not required to be diagnosed.

Examples

In general, a translation unit shall contain no more than one definition of any class type. In this example, two definitions of the class type C occur in the same translation unit. This typically occurs if a header file is included twice by the same source file without appropriate header guards.

```
class C {}; // first definition of C
class C {}; // error, second definition
of C
```

In the following, forming a pointer to S or defining a function taking a reference to S are examples of legal constructs, because they do not require the type of S to be complete. Therefore, a definition is not required.

Defining an object of type S, a function taking an argument of type S, or using S in a sizeof expression are examples of contexts where S must be complete, and therefore require a definition.

```
struct S;  // declaration of S
S * p;     // ok, no definition required
void f(S&); // ok, no definition required
void f(S);  // ok, no definition required
S f();     // ok, no definition required

S s;       // error, definition required
sizeof(S); // error, definition required
```

More than one definition

In certain cases, there can be more than one definition of a type or a template. A program consisting of multiple header files and source files will typically have more than one definition of a type, but not more than one definition per translation unit.

If a program contains more than one definition of a type, then each definition must be equivalent.

Definitions of static const data members

In pre-standard C++, all static data members required a definition outside of their class. However, during the C++ standardization process it was decided to lift this requirement for static const integral members. The intent was to allow uses such as:

```
struct C
{
  static const int N = 10;
};
char data[C::N]; // N "used" without
out-of-class definition
```

without a namespace scope definition for N.

Nevertheless, the wording of the 1998 C++ standard still required a definition if the member was used in the program. This included the member appearing anywhere except as the operand to sizeof or typeid, effectively making the above ill-formed.

This was identified as a defect, and the wording was adjusted to allow such a member to appear anywhere a constant expression is required, without requiring an out-of-class definition. This includes array bounds, case expressions, static member initializers, and nontype template arguments.

```
struct C
{
  static const int N = 10;
  static const int U = N; // Legal per C+
+03
};

char data[C::N]; // Legal per C++03

template<int> struct D;

template<> struct D<C::N> {}; //
Legal per C++03
```

However, using a static const integral member anywhere except where an integral constant-expression is required requires a definition:

```
struct C
{
  static const int N = 10;
};

int main()
{
  int i = C::N; // ill-formed, definition
of C::N required
}
```

This requirement will be relaxed in the upcoming C++ standard, colloquially referred to as C++0x.

Source (edited): "http://en.wikipedia.org/wiki/One_Definition_Rule"

Opaque pointer

In computer programming, an **opaque pointer** is a special case of opaque data type, a datatype that is declared to be a pointer to a record or data structure of some unspecified type.

Opaque pointers are present in several programming languages including Ada, C, C++ and Modula-2.

If the language is strongly typed, programs and procedures that have no other information about an opaque pointer type *T* can still declare variables, arrays, and record fields of type *T*, assign values of that type, and compare those values for equality. However, they will not be able to de-reference such a pointer, and can only change the object's content by calling some procedure that has the missing information.

Opaque pointers are a way to hide the implementation details of an interface from ordinary clients, so that the implementation may be changed without the need to recompile the modules using it. This benefits the programmer as well since a simple interface can be created, and most details can be hidden in another file. This is important for providing binary code compatibility through different versions of a shared library, for example.

This technique is sometimes referred to as "**handle classes**", the "**Pimpl idiom**" (for "pointer to implementation idiom"), "**Compiler firewall idiom**" or "**Cheshire Cat**", especially among the C++ community.

Examples

Ada

```
package Library_Interface is

  type Handle is limited private;

  -- Operations...

private
  type Hidden_Implementation;    -- Defined in the package body
  type Handle is access Hidden_Implementation;
end Library_Interface;
```

The type Handle is an opaque pointer to the real implementation, that is not defined in the specification. Note that the type is not only private (to forbid the clients from accessing the type directly, and only through the operations), but also limited (to avoid the copy of the data structure, and thus preventing dangling references).

```
package body Library_Interface is

  type Hidden_Implementation is record
    ...  -- The actual implementation can be anything
  end record;

  -- Definition of the operations...

end Library_Interface;
```

These types are sometimes called "**Taft types**"—named after Tucker Taft, the main designer of Ada 95—because they were introduced in the so-called Taft Amendment to Ada 83.

C

```
/* cat.h */
typedef struct cat_t *cat_handle;

/*
 * Even though the compiler doesn't know anything about the struct
 * at this point, it can use a pointer to that struct.
 */

/*
 * This function creates a cat object with the given smile value.
 * A result of NULL indicates an error.
 */
cat_handle cat_Create(int smile);

/*
 * This function destroys a cat object.
 * If called with NULL, no action is taken.
 */
void cat_Destroy(cat_handle cat);

/*
 * This function sets the smile value of a cat object to the
 * new value, and returns the old value.
 * A result of -1 indicates an error.
 */
int cat_Smile(cat_handle cat, int newsmile);
```

```
/* cat.c */
#include "cat.h"
#include <stdlib.h>

struct cat_t {
  int smile;
};

/* Create a cat object */
cat_handle cat_Create(int smile) {
  cat_handle result = malloc(sizeof(struct cat_t));

  if (result) {
    result->smile = smile;
  }

  return result;
}

/* Destroy a cat object */
void cat_Destroy(cat_handle cat) {
  free(cat);
}

/* Set the smile value of a cat */
int cat_Smile(cat_handle cat, int newsmile) {
  if (cat) {
    int t = cat->smile;
    cat->smile = newsmile;
    return t;
  }

  return -1;
}
```

This example demonstrates a way to achieve the information hiding (encapsulation) aspect of Object-Oriented Programming using the C language. If someone wanted to change the declaration of struct cat_t, it would be unnecessary to recompile any other modules in the program that use the cat.h header file unless the API was also changed.

C++

In the example below, the copy assignment operator takes its argument by value, eliminating the need to explicitly create a copy of the other object.

```
//header file:
class Handle {
private:
   struct CheshireCat;          // Not defined here
   CheshireCat *smile;          // Handle

public:
   Handle();                    // Constructor
   Handle(const Handle& );      // Copy constructor
   Handle& operator=(Handle);   // Copy assignment operator
   ~Handle();                   // Destructor
   // Other operations...
};
```

```
//CPP file:
#include "handle.h"

struct Handle::CheshireCat {
   // The actual implementation can be anything
   // ...
};

Handle::Handle()
   : smile( new CheshireCat ) {
   // do nothing
}

Handle::Handle(const Handle& other)
   : smile( new CheshireCat(*(other.smile))) {
   // do nothing
}

Handle &Handle::operator=(Handle other) {
   std::swap( this->smile, other.smile );
   return *this;
}

Handle::~Handle() {
   delete smile;
}
```

One type of opaque pointer commonly used in C++ class declarations is the d-pointer. The d-pointer is the only private data member of the class and points to an instance of a struct (which must be a POD since its destructor is not visible) defined in the class' implementation file. Named by Arnt Gulbrandsen of Trolltech, this method allows class declarations to omit private data members, except for the d-pointer itself. The result is that more of the class' implementation is hidden from view, that adding new data members to the private struct does not affect binary compatibility, and that the header file containing the class declaration only has to #include those other files that are needed for the class interface, rather than for its implementation. As a side benefit, compiles are faster because the header file changes less often. The d-pointer is heavily used in the Qt and KDE libraries.

C#

See Private class data pattern

Source (edited): "http://en.wikipedia.org/wiki/Opaque_pointer"

OpenC++ (software tool)

OpenC++ is a software tool to parse and analyze C++ source code. It uses a metaobject protocol (MOP) to provide services for language extensions. OpenC++ got its continuation in VivaCore library .

Source (edited): "http://en.wikipedia.org/wiki/OpenC%2B%2B_(software_tool)"

Operators in C and C++

This is a list of operators in the C and C ++ programming languages. All the operators listed exist in C++; the fourth column "Included in C", dictates whether an operator is also present in C. Note that C does not support operator overloading.

When not overloaded, for the operators **&&**, ||, and **,** (the comma operator), there is a sequence point after the evaluation of the first operand.

C++ also contains the type conversion operators **const_cast**, **static_cast**, **dynamic_cast**, and **reinterpret_cast** which are not listed in the table for brevity. The formatting of these operators means that their precedence level is unimportant.

Most of the operators available in C and C++ are also available in other languages such as C#, Java, Perl, and PHP with the same precedence, associativity, and semantics.

Table

For the purposes of this table, a, b, and c represent valid values (literals, values from variables, or return value), object names, or lvalues, as appropriate.

Overloadable means that the operator is overloadable in C++. "Included in C" means that the operator exists and has a semantic meaning in C (operators are not overloadable in C).

Notes:

Operator precedence

The following is a table that lists the precedence and associativity of all the operators in the C and C++ languages (when the operators also exist in Java, Perl, PHP and many other recent languages, the precedence is the same as that given). Operators are listed top to bottom, in descending precedence.

Descending precedence refers to the priority of evaluation. Considering an expression, an operator which is listed on some row will be evaluated prior to any operator that is listed on a row further below it. Operators that are in the same cell (there may be several rows of operators listed in a cell) are evaluated with the same precedence, in the given direction. An operator's precedence is unaffected by overloading.

The syntax of expressions in C and C++ is specified by a context-free grammar. The table given here has been inferred from the grammar. For the ISO C 1999 standard, section 6.5.6 note 71 states that the C grammar provided by the specification defines the precedence of the C operators, and also states that the operator precedence resulting from the grammar closely follows the specification's section ordering:

"The [C] syntax [i.e., grammar] specifies the precedence of operators in the evaluation of an expression, which is the same as the order of the major subclauses of this subclause, highest precedence first."

A precedence table, while mostly adequate, cannot resolve a few details. In particular, note that the ternary operator allows any arbitrary expression as its middle operand, despite being listed as having higher precedence than the assignment and comma operators. Thus a ? b , c : d is interpreted as a ? (b, c) : d, and not as the meaningless (a ? b), (c : d). Also, note that the immediate, unparenthesized result of a C cast expression cannot be the operand of sizeof. Therefore, sizeof (int) * x is interpreted as (sizeof(int)) * x and not sizeof ((int) *x).

Source (edited): "http://en.wikipedia.org/wiki/Operators_in_C_and_C%2B%2B"

POCO C++ Libraries

The **POCO C++ Libraries** are a collection of open source class libraries for developing network-centric, portable applications in C++. POCO stands for **POrtable COmponents**. The libraries cover functionality such as threads, thread synchronization, file system access, streams, shared libraries and class loading, sockets and network protocols (HTTP, FTP, SMTP, etc.), and include an HTTP server, as well as an XML parser with SAX2 and DOM interfaces and SQL database access. The modular and efficient design and implementation makes the POCO C++ Libraries well suited for embedded development.

Overview

POCO is a collection of C++ libraries providing users with library support similar to that found in other development environments, like the Java Class Library, the .NET Framework or Apple's Cocoa. POCO is centered around network-centric application domains and developed with modern ANSI/ISO Standard C++ and C++ Standard Library facilities and techniques with emphasis on powerful functionality, ease of use, and consistency. Governed primarily by code quality, consistent style and unit testing POCO is highly portable Open Source software already ported to a variety of different platforms while being released under the Boost Software License.

Hierarchy of POCO C++ Libraries

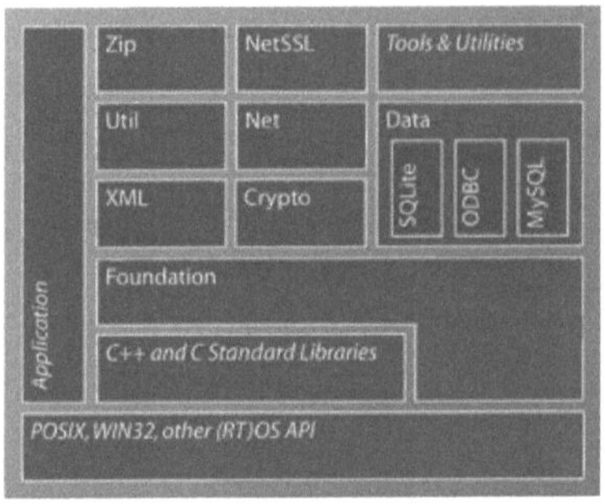

POCO C++ Libraries are currently split into four core libraries with optional add-on libraries available with each release. The design and hierarchy of POCO C++ is considered well designed . The four core component libraries cover the following areas that can be found in the economy package:

Foundation

- Platform abstraction - Eases porting issues of fundamental types, etc.
- Memory management - RAII, auto_ptr, reference counting garbage collection, etc.
- String utilities
- Error handling - Extended exception classes
- streams - Encoding and decoding and filtering support
- threads - Concurrent processing support
- Date and time - Date and time support including formatting and high precision timers
- File system - Abstracted file system support
- Logging - Application and system logging, filtering and logging strategies
- Processes - Interprocess communication and memory sharing
- shared libraries - Dynamic library support
- Notifications - Abstracted notification support
- Events - Abstracted event support and strategies
- Crypt - Random number generation, Digests and encoding/decoding engines
- Text - Unicode encoding support
- Regular expressions - Based on Perl compatible regular expression
- URI - Universal Resource Identifier support
- UUID - Universally Unique Identifiers support and generators
- Cache support - Abstracted strategy support

Net

- sockets - Abstracted low level network support
- Reactor pattern - Popular network abstraction pattern support
- MIME messages - Encoding support
- HTTP - High level HTTP support for client and servers
- FTP - High level FTP support
- Mail - POP3, SMTP stream based

- support
- HTML - Form support

XML

- SAX2
- DOM
- XML writer

Util

- Configuration files
- Command line options
- Tools and server application framework

One design goal of a many targeted decisions are based around POCO C++ providing an easy to use component library that works out of the box. POCO C++ Libraries are currently available in two package formats. These formats are the economy and the complete edition. While the complete edition covers NetSSL, Crypto, Zip and Data capabilities among others, the economy package does not and thus eliminates the dependence on external facilities such as OpenSSL, ODBC and MySQL dependencies.

The open source nature of POCO enables and encourages development of additional library functionality. Design and development of existing and upcoming library support is driven by the pragmatic needs of the user base. Library additions take place in a sandbox development environment and are reviewed and integrated into the main library releases as approved by the core development team with input from contributors.

History

- 2004 - Günter Obiltschnig started POCO with the development of the class libraries as the result of being dissatisfied by what was available in C++ class libraries for network centric programming.
- February 21, 2005 - The first public release on Sourceforge, which contained the Foundation and XML support libraries. POCO was released under the Sleepycat license at the time.
- May 2005 - Aleksandar Fabijanic made the first contribution.
- January 19, 2006 - POCO 1.0 was released, including the Net library.
- July 2006 - POCO was re-licensed under the Boost license.
- May 2007 - POCO 1.3 was released, including the Data library
- December 2010 - POCO 1.4 was released, including many improvements.

POCO C++ Libraries Users

- Appcelerator Titanium
- Schneider Electric Buildings (formerly TAC)
- CACE Technologies
- Mantid
- Medical Imaging Interaction Toolkit
- OpenFrameworks
- GLUEscript
- SeguriData
- Aysso Systems
- Tonido

Source (edited): "http://en.wikipedia.org/wiki/POCO_C%2B%2B_Libraries"

Partial template specialization

Partial template specialization is a particular form of class template specialization. Usually used in reference to the C++ programming language, it allows the programmer to specialize only some arguments of a class template, as opposed to explicit specialization, where all the template arguments are provided.

Templates and specialization

Class templates are really meta-classes: they are partial abstract data types that provide instructions to the compiler on how to create classes with the proper data members. For example, the C++ standard containers are class templates. When a programmer uses a vector, one instantiates it with a specific data type, for example, int, string or double. Each type of vector results in a different class in the compiler's object code, each one working with a different data type.

If one knows that a class template will be used with a specific data type fairly often and this data type allows some optimizations (e.g. bit shifting with integers, as opposed to multiplying or dividing by 2), one may specialize the template by specifying another class template that is identical but by specifying the parameter types. When the compiler sees such a class template instantiated in code, it will generally choose the most specialized template definition that matches the instantiation. Therefore, an explicit specialization (one where all the template arguments are specified) will be preferred to a partial specialization if all the template arguments match.

Partial specialization

Templates can have more than one parameter type. Some older compilers allow one only to specialize either all or none of the template's parameters. Compilers that support partial specialization allow the programmer to specialize some parameters while leaving the others generic. Until recently most compilers did not support this feature well (at best) or ignored such specializations (at worst).

At least the GNU, Intel, Comeau, and Microsoft compilers fully support partial specialization of templates.

Source (edited): "http://en.wikipedia.org/wiki/Partial_template_specialization"

Pete Becker

Pete Becker is one of the world's foremost C++ experts. He is known primarily for his book, *The C++ Standard Library Extensions: A Tutorial and Reference*, and his involvement in the C++ standardization process.

Career

Becker worked for eight years at Borland International as a quality assurance engineer and manager, library implementor, and development manager. From 1997 to 2005 he was employed at Dinkumware, working on the source code and documentation of their C++ Standard Library and C Standard Library implementations.

C++ Standards Committee

Becker has been a member of the ISO/IEC (JTC1/SC22/WG21) C++ Standards committee since its inception in 1991. His work includes a proposal for standard support of dynamic libraries in C++. He is currently the Project Editor. His tasks include maintaining the working draft of the constantly evolving C++ standards document for the upcoming C++ standard, colloquially referred to as C++0x.

Source (edited): "http://en.wikipedia.org/wiki/Pete_Becker"

Placement syntax

In the C++ programming language, **placement syntax** allows programmers to explicitly specify the memory management of individual objects — i.e. their "placement" in memory. Normally, when an object is created dynamically, an allocation function is invoked in such a way that it will both allocate memory for the object, and initialize the object within the newly allocated memory. The placement syntax allows the programmer to supply additional arguments to the allocation function. A common use is to supply a pointer to a suitable region of storage where the object can be initialized, thus separating memory allocation from object construction.

The "placement" versions of the new and delete operators and functions are known as placement new and placement delete. A new *expression*, placement or otherwise, calls a new *function*, also known as an allocator function, whose name is operator new. Similarly, a delete *expression* calls a delete *function*, also known as a deallocator function, whose name is operator delete.

Any new expression that uses the placement syntax is a placement new expression, and any operator new or operator delete function that takes more than the mandatory first parameter (size_t and void *, respectively) is a placement new or placement delete function.

History

In earlier versions of C++ there was no such thing as *placement new*; instead, developers used explicit assignment to *this* within constructors to achieve similar effect. This practice has been deprecated and abolished later, and third edition of *The C++ Programming Language* doesn't mention this technique. Support for *placement new* operator has been added to compilers circa 1995.

Expressions

The Standard C++ syntax for a non-placement new expression is

new *new-type-id* (*optional-initializer-expression-list*)

The placement syntax adds an expression list immediately after the new keyword. This expression list is the placement. It can contain any number of expressions.

new (*expression-list*) *new-type-id* (*optional-initializer-expression-list*)

There is no placement delete expression.

Functions

The placement new functions are overloads of the non-placement new functions. The declaration of the non-placement new functions, for non-array and array new expressions respectively, are:

void * operator new (size_t) throw(std::bad_alloc);

void * operator new[] (size_t) throw(std::bad_alloc);

The Standard C++ library provides two placement overloads each for these functions. Their declarations are:

void * operator new (size_t, const std::nothrow_t &) throw();

void * operator new (size_t, void *) throw();

void * operator new[] (size_t, const std::nothrow_t &) throw();

void * operator new[] (size_t, void *) throw();

In all of the overloads, the first parameter to the operator new function is of type size_t, which when the function is called will be passed as an argument the amount of memory, in bytes, to allocate. All of the functions must return type void *, which is a pointer to the storage that the function allocates.

There are also placement delete functions. They are overloaded versions of the non-placement delete functions. The non-placement delete functions are declared as:

void operator delete (void *) throw();

void operator delete[] (void *) throw();

The Standard C++ library provides two placement overloads each for these functions. Their declarations are:

void operator delete (void *, const std::nothrow_t &) throw();

void operator delete (void *, void *) throw();

void operator delete[] (void *, const std::nothrow_t &) throw();

void operator delete[] (void *, void *) throw();

In all of the overloads, the first parameter to the operator delete function is of type void *, which is the address of the storage to deallocate.

For both the new and the delete functions, the functions are global, are not in any namespace, and do not have static linkage.

Use

Placement syntax has four main uses: default placement, preventing exceptions, custom allocators, and debugging.

Default placement

The placement overloads of operator new and operator delete that employ an additional void * parameter are used for default placement, also known as *pointer placement*. Their definitions by the

Standard C++ library, which it is not permitted for a C++ program to replace or override, are:

```
void * operator new (size_t, void * p) throw() { return p ; }
void * operator new[] (size_t, void * p) throw() { return p ; }
void operator delete (void *, void *) throw() { }
void operator delete[] (void *, void *) throw() { }
```

Default placement does not require the inclusion of the Standard C++ library header <new> in the source code of a C++ program. However, g++ version 4.0 still requires the use of this header (this might be true of other versions of the compiler or other compilers too.)

There are various uses for default placement.

Bjarne Stroustrup originally observed, in his book *The Design and Evolution of C++*, that pointer placement new is necessary for hardware that expects a certain object at a specific hardware address. It is also required for the construction of objects that need to reside in a certain memory area, such as an area that is shared between several processors of a multiprocessor computer.

Other uses, however, include calling a constructor directly, something which the C++ language does not otherwise permit.

The C++ language does allow a program to call a destructor directly, and, since it is not possible to destroy the object using a delete expression, that is how one destroys an object that was constructed via a pointer placement new expression. For example:

```
p->~T() ;
```

Preventing exceptions

Normally, the (non-placement) new functions throw an exception, of type std::bad_alloc, if they encounter an error, such as exhaustion of all available memory. This was not how the functions were defined by Stroustrup's *Annotated C++ Reference Manual*, but was a change made by the standardization committee when the C++ language was standardized. The original behaviour of the functions, which was to return a NULL pointer when an error occurred, is accessible via placement syntax.

Programmers who wish to do this in their programs must include the Standard C++ library header <new> in the source code. This header declares the global std::nothrow object, which is of type std::nothrow_t (also declared in the header), which is used to call the overloaded new functions that are declared as taking const nothrow_t & as their second parameter. For example:

```
#include <new>

struct T {} ;

int main ()
{
  // Call the function operator new(size_t, const nothrow_t &) and (if successful) construct the object.
  T * p = new (std::nothrow) T ;
  if (p) {
     // The storage has been allocated and the constructor called.
     delete p ;
  } else
     ; // An error has occurred. No storage has been allocated and no object constructed.
  return 0 ;
}
```

Custom allocators

Placement syntax is also employed for custom allocators. This does not use any of the allocator and deallocator functions from the Standard C++ library header <new>, but requires that programmers write their own allocation and deallocation functions, overloaded for user-defined types. For example, one could define a memory management class as follows:

```
#include <cstdlib>
class A {
public:
  void * allocate ( size_t ) ;
  void deallocate ( void * ) ;
} ;
```

And define custom placement allocation and deallocation functions as follows:

```
void *
operator new (size_t size, A & arena)
{
  return arena.allocate(size) ;
}
void
operator delete (void * p, A & arena)
{
  arena.deallocate(p) ;
}
```

The program would employ the placement syntax to allocate objects using different instances of the A class as follows:

```
A first_arena, second_arena ;
T * p1 = new (first_arena) T ;
T * p2 = new (second_arena) T ;
```

Destroying an object whose storage is allocated in such a fashion requires some care. Because there is no placement delete expression, one cannot use it to invoke the custom deallocator. One must either write a destruction function that invokes the custom deallocator, or call the placement delete function directly, as a function call.

The former would resemble:

```
void
destroy (T * p, A & arena)
{
  p->~T() ; // First invoke the destructor explicitly.
  arena.deallocate(p) ; // Then call the deallocator function directly.
}
```

which would be invoked from a program as:

```
A arena ;
T * p = new (arena) T ;
/* ... */
destroy(p, arena) ;
```

The latter would involve simply writing the destructor invocation and delete function call into the program:

```
A arena ;
T * p = new (arena) T ;
/* ... */
p->~T() ;   // First invoke the destructor explicitly.
operator delete(p, arena) ;  // Then call the deallocator function indirectly via operator delete(void *, A &) .
```

A common error is to attempt to use a delete expression to delete the object. This results in the wrong operator delete function being called. Dewhurst recommends two strategies for avoiding this error. The first is to ensure that any custom allocators rely upon the Standard C++ library's global, non-placement, operator new, and are thus nothing more than simple wrappers around the C++ library's memory management. The second is to create new and delete functions for individual classes, and customize memory management via class function members rather than by using the placement syntax.

Debugging

Placement new can also be used as a simple debugging tool, to enable programs to print the filename and line number of the source code where a memory allocation has failed. This does not require the inclusion of the Standard C++ library header <new>, but does require the inclusion of a header that declares four placement functions and a macro replacement for the new keyword that is used in new expressions. For example, such a header would contain:

```
#if defined(DEBUG_NEW)
void * operator new (size_t size, const char* file, int line);
void * operator new[] (size_t size, const char* file, int line);
void operator delete (void * p, const char* file, int line);
void operator delete[] (void * p, const char* file, int line);
#define New new(__FILE__, __LINE__)
#else
#define New new
#endif
```

This would be employed in a program as follows:

```
T * p = New T ;
```

The custom-written placement new functions would then handle using the supplied file and line number information in the event of an exception. For example:

```
#include <new>
#include <cstdlib>

class NewError {
public:
  NewError(const char * file, int line) { /* ... */ }
  /* ... */
} ;

void *
operator new (size_t size, const char* file, int line)
{
   if (void * p = ::operator new (size, std::nothrow))
      return p ;
  throw NewError(file, line) ;
}
```

Placement delete

As noted above, there is no placement delete expression. It is not possible to call *any* placement operator delete function using a delete expression.

The placement delete functions are called from placement new expressions. In particular, they are called if the constructor of the object throws an exception. In such a circumstance, in order to ensure that the program does not incur a memory leak, the placement delete functions are called. A placement new expression first calls the placement operator new function, then calls the constructor of the object upon the raw storage returned from the allocator function. If the constructor throws an exception, it is necessary to deallocate that storage before propagating the exception back to the code that executed the placement new expression, and that is the purpose of the placement delete functions.

The placement delete function that is called matches the placement new function that was invoked by the placement new expression. So, for example, if the following code is executed, the placement delete function that is called will be operator delete(void *, const A &):

```
#include <cstdlib>

struct A {} ;
struct E {} ;

class T {
public:
   T() { throw E() ; }
} ;

void * operator new ( size_t, const A & ) ;
void operator delete ( void *, const A & ) ;

int main ()
{
   A a ;
   T * p = new (a) T ;
   return 0 ;
}
```

This is why the *pointer placement* delete functions are defined as no-operations by the Standard C++ library. Since the pointer placement new functions do not allocate any storage, there is no storage to be deallocated in the event of the object's constructor throwing an exception.

If no matching placement delete function exists, no deallocation function is called in the event of an exception being thrown by a constructor within a placement new expression. There are also some (older) C++ implementations that do not support placement delete (which, like the exception-throwing allocator functions, were an addition made to C++ when it was standardized) at all. In both such situations, an exception being thrown by a constructor when allocating using a custom allocator will result in a memory leak. (In the case of the older C++ implementations, a memory leak will also occur with *non*-placement new expressions.)

Source (edited): "http://en.wikipedia.org/wiki/Placement_syntax"

Plain Old C++ Object

Like the term *plain old Java object (POJO)* in the Java world, the term ***Plain Old C/C++ object*** or its acronym ***POCO*** means a C/C++ artifact that is *neither defined by nor coupled to* the underlying C/C++ component framework that manipulates it. Examples of such an artifact include, for instance, instances of a C++ classes, K&R structs, unions, or even functions (as function pointers). This is contrast to component model in classic C/C++ component frameworks, such as OMG-CCM, JTRS-SCA core framework (CF), OpenSOA's SCA for C++. These classic component frameworks either dedicate a proprietary component programming model (a super class), or mandate component implementations to be tightly coupled to the underlying framework (calling its runtime).

Source (edited): "http://en.wikipedia.org/wiki/Plain_Old_C%2B%2B_Object"

Plain old data structure

A **plain old data structure (POD)** is a data structure that is represented only as passive collections of field values, without using encapsulation or other object-oriented features.

Plain old data structures are appropriate when there is a part of a system where it should be clearly indicated that the detailed logic for data manipulation and integrity are elsewhere. PODs are often found at the boundaries of a system, where information is being moved to and from other systems or persistent storage and the business logic that is found in other parts of the system is not relevant. For example, PODs would be convenient for representing the field values of objects that are being constructed from external data, in a part of the system where the semantic checks and interpretations needed for valid objects have not yet been applied.

A POD type in C++ is defined as either a scalar type or a POD class. A POD class has no user-defined copy assignment operator, no user-defined destructor, and no non-static data members that are not themselves PODs. Moreover, a POD class must be an aggregate, meaning it has no user-declared constructors, no private nor protected non-static data, no base classes and no virtual functions. The standard includes statements about how PODs must behave in C++.

In certain contexts, C++ allows only POD types to be used. For example, a union in C++ cannot contain a class that has virtual functions or nontrivial constructors or destructors. This restriction is imposed because the compiler cannot know which constructor or destructor should be called for a union. POD types can also be used for interfacing with C, which supports only PODs.

In Java, some developers consider that the POD concept corresponds to a class with public data members and no methods, i.e., a data transfer object. Others would consider it a class that has methods but only getters and setters, with no logic. Java Beans fall under the POD concept if they do not use event handling and do not implement additional methods beyond getters and setters.

Other structured data representations such as XML can also be used as PODs if no significant semantic restrictions are used.

Source (edited): "http://en.wikipedia.org/wiki/Plain_old_data_structure"

pragma once

In the C and C++ programming languages, **#pragma once** is a non-standard but widely supported preprocessor directive designed to cause the current source file to be included only once in a single compilation. Thus, #pragma once serves the same purpose as #include guards, but with several advantages, including: less code, avoiding name clashes, and improved compile speed.

See the article on #include guards for an example of a situation in which one or the other of these methods must be used. The solution using include guards is given on that page; the #pragma once solution would be:

File "grandfather.h"

```
#pragma once

struct foo
{
  int member;
};
```

File "father.h"

```
#include "grandfather.h"
```

File "child.c"

```
#include "grandfather.h"
#include "father.h"
```

Advantages and disadvantages

Using #pragma once instead of include guards will typically increase compilation speed since it is a higher-level mechanism; the compiler itself can compare filenames or inodes without having to invoke the C preprocessor to scan the header for #ifndef and #endif.

Some compilers such as GCC include special speedup code to recognize and optimize the handling of include guards, and thus little or no speedup benefit is obtained from the use of #pragma once.

Again because the compiler itself is responsible for handling #pragma once, it is not necessary for the programmer to create new macro names such as GRANDFATHER_H in the Include guard article's example. This eliminates the risk of name clashes, meaning that no header file can *fail* to be included at least once. It also requires less typing than the include guard method.

However, this high-level handling is

not perfect; the programmer must rely on the compiler to handle #pragma once correctly. If the compiler makes a mistake, for example by failing to recognize that two symbolic links with different names point to the same file, then the compilation will fail. Compilers with #pragma once-related bugs included LCC-Win32 as of 2004 and GCC as of 1998. GCC originally gave a warning declaring #pragma once "obsolete" when compiling code that used it. However, with the 3.4 release of GCC, the #pragma once handling code was fixed to behave correctly with symbolic and hard links. The feature was "un-deprecated" and the warning removed.

Both #pragma once and include guards can be used to write portable code that can also take advantage of #pragma once optimizations the compiler may support:

File "grandfather.h"

```
#pragma once
#ifndef GRANDFATHER_H
#define GRANDFATHER_H

struct foo
{
  int member;
};

#endif /* GRANDFATHER_H */
```

Source (edited): "http://en.wikipedia.org/wiki/Pragma_once"

Precompiled header

In computer programming, a **pre-compiled header** is a technique used by some C or C++ compilers to reduce compilation time.

Overview

In the C and C++ programming languages, a header file is a file whose text may be automatically included in another source file by the C preprocessor, usually specified by the use of compiler directives in the source file.

Header files can sometimes contain a very large amount of source code (for instance, the header files windows.h and Cocoa/Cocoa.h on Microsoft Windows and Mac OS X, respectively).

To reduce compilation times some compilers allow header files to be pre-compiled into a form that is faster for the compiler to process. This intermediate form is known as a *precompiled header*, and is commonly held in a file named with the extensions .pch or .gch.

A related feature is the prefix header, which is a file that is automatically included by the compiler without requiring the use of any compiler directives. Prefix headers are commonly precompiled, but not all precompiled headers are prefix headers.

Usage

Simple Example

Given a C++ file source.cpp that includes header.hpp:

```
// header.hpp
...


// source.cpp
#include "header.hpp"
...
```

When compiling source.cpp for the first time with the pre-compiled header feature turned on, the compiler will generate a pre-compiled header, header.pch. The next time, the compiler can skip the compilation phase relating to header.hpp and instead use header.pch directly.

Example with forward declaration

We have two classes A (in A.h and A.cpp) and B (in B.h and B.cpp). Class A is quite simple:

```
class A {
  ...
};
```

When class B is composed by an attribute of class A, normally the class A will become part of the class:

```
#include "A.h"
class B1 {
  ...
  A mA;
};
```

To prevent recompilation of B1.h, when class A changes, sometimes pointer syntax will be used; B2.h:

```
class A;
class B2 {
  ...
  A* mA;
};
```

As can be seen, a forward declaration of class A is used instead of including the header. But this pointer syntax complicates the usage of the variable as price for lesser compilation.

This problem can be solved by the usage of pre-compiled headers. We can use the easier syntax in B1.h and advise the compiler to use pre-compiled headers. Then the files A.pch and B1.pch will be created.

When the class A is changed now, only A.h has to be parsed again and written to the pre-compiled header A.pch. As the file B1.h is not changed, it does not need to be parsed again and the already existing pre-compiled header B1.pch can be used.

Common Implementations

stdafx.h

stdafx.h is a file, generated by Microsoft Visual Studio IDE wizards, that describes both standard system and project specific include files that are used frequently but hardly ever change.

Compatible compilers (for example,

Visual C++ 6.0 and newer) will pre-compile this file to reduce overall compile times. Visual C++ will not compile anything before the #include "stdafx.h" in the source file, unless the compile option /Yu'stdafx.h' is unchecked (by default); it assumes all code in the source up to and including that line is already compiled.

The AFX in stdafx.h stands for Application Framework eXtensions. AFX was the original abbreviation for the Microsoft Foundation Classes (MFC). Optionally, Visual Studio projects may avoid pre-compiled headers, as well as they may specify an alternative name (though **stdafx.h** is used by default).

GCC

Pre-compiled headers are supported in GCC (3.4 and newer). GCC's approach is similar to these of VC and compatible compilers. GCC saves the pre-compiled version using a ".gch" suffix. When compiling source files, the compiler checks whether those files are present. If possible, the pre-compiled version is used. If this is not possible, then, the normal header is still present as a fall-back plan.

GCC can only use the pre-compiled version if the same compiler switches are set as when the header was compiled and it may use at most one. Further, only preprocessor instructions may be placed before the pre-compiled header (because it must be directly or indirectly included through another normal header, before any compilable code).

GCC automatically identifies most header files using their extension. However, if this fails (e.g. because of non standard header extensions), the -x switch can be used to be sure that GCC treats the file as a header instead of a normal source file.

C++Builder

In the default project configuration, the C++Builder compiler implicitly generates precompiled headers for all headers included by a source module until the line #pragma hdrstop is found. Precompiled headers are shared for all modules of the project if possible. For example, when working with the Visual Component Library, it is common to include the <vcl.h> header first which contains most of the commonly used VCL header files. Thus, the precompiled header can be shared across all project modules, which dramatically reduces the build times.

In addition, C++Builder can be instrumented to use a specific header file as precompiled header, similar to the mechanism provided by Visual C++.

C++Builder 2009 introduces a "Precompiled Header Wizard" which parses all source modules of the project for included header files, classifies them (i.e. excludes header files if they are part of the project or do not have an Include guard) and generates and tests a precompiled header for the specified files automatically.

Source (edited): "http://en.wikipedia.org/wiki/Precompiled_header"

Prefix header

In computer programming, a **prefix header** is a feature found in some C or C++ compilers used to simplify code and/or to reduce compilation time.

Overview

In the C and C++ programming languages, a header file is a file whose text is automatically included in another source file by the compiler, usually by the use of compiler directives at the beginning of the source file. A prefix header differs from a normal header file in that it is *automatically* included at the beginning of every source file by the compiler, without the use of any compiler directives.

Prefix headers are usually pre-compiled in order to reduce compilation times.

Example

On Mac OS X, the Xcode build system generates prefix headers automatically for new projects. A new Cocoa project, for instance, gets a prefix header that looks like this:

```
#ifdef __OBJC__
  #import <Cocoa/Cocoa.h>
#endif
```

As a result, it is unnecessary to explicitly include any of the above files in any Objective-C code in the program, although doing so is harmless, in the case of Objective-C because of the semantics of the #import directive, but more generally with #include because of the use of include guards.

Similar prefix headers are generated for other types of project.

Source (edited): "http://en.wikipedia.org/wiki/Prefix_header"

Pro*C

Pro*C (also known as **Pro*C/C++**) is an embedded SQL programming language used by Oracle Database and Sybase SQL Server database management systems. Pro*C uses either C or C++ as its host language. During compilation, the embedded SQL statements are interpreted by a precompiler and replaced by C or C++ function calls to their respective SQL library. The output from the Pro*C precompiler is standard C or C++ code that is then compiled by any one of several C or C++ compilers into an executable.

Source (edited): "http://en.wikipedia.

org/wiki/Pro*C"

Reference (C++)

In the C++ programming language, a **reference** is a simple reference datatype that is less powerful but safer than the pointer type inherited from C. The name *C++ reference* may cause confusion, as in computer science a reference is a general concept datatype, with *pointers* and *C++ references* being specific reference datatype implementations.

Syntax and terminology

The declaration of the form:

<Type> & <Name>

where <Type> is a type and <Name> is an identifier whose type is **reference to <Type>**.

Examples:

- int A = 5;
- int& rA = A;
- extern int& rB;
- int& foo ();
- void bar (int& rP);
- class MyClass { int& m_b; /* ... */ };
- int funcX() { return 42 ; }; int (&xFunc)() = funcX;

Here, rA and rB are of type "reference to int", foo() is a function that returns a reference to int, bar() is a function with a reference parameter, which is reference to int, MyClass is a class with a member which is reference to int, funcX() is a function that returns an int, xFunc() is an alias for funcX.

Types which are of kind "reference to <Type>" are sometimes called **reference types**. Identifiers which are of reference type are called **reference variables**. To call them *variable*, however, is in fact a misnomer, as we will see.

Relationship to pointers

C++ references differ from pointers in several essential ways:

- It is not possible to refer directly to a reference object after it is defined; any occurrence of its name refers directly to the object it references.
- Once a reference is created, it cannot be later made to reference another object; it cannot be *reseated*. This is often done with pointers.
- References cannot be *null*, whereas pointers can; every reference refers to some object, although it may or may not be valid.
- References cannot be uninitialized. Because it is impossible to reinitialize a reference, they must be initialized as soon as they are created. In particular, local and global variables must be initialized where they are defined, and references which are data members of class instances must be initialized in the initializer list of the class's constructor. For example:

int& k; // compiler will complain: error: `k' declared as reference but not initialized

- Most compilers will support a null reference without much complaint, crashing only if you try to use the reference in some way.

There is a simple conversion between pointers and references: the address-of operator (&) will yield a pointer referring to the same object when applied to a reference, and a reference which is initialized from the dereference (*) of a pointer value will refer to the same object as that pointer, where this is possible without invoking undefined behavior. This equivalence is a reflection of the typical implementation, which effectively compiles references into pointers which are implicitly dereferenced at each use.

A consequence of this is that in many implementations, operating on a variable with automatic or static lifetime through a reference, although syntactically similar to accessing it directly, can involve hidden dereference operations that are costly. References are a syntactically controversial feature of C++ because they obscure an identifier's level of indirection; that is, unlike C code where pointers usually stand out syntactically, in a large block of C++ code it may not be immediately obvious if the object being accessed is defined as a local or global variable or whether it is a reference (implicit pointer) to some other location, especially if the code mixes references and pointers. This aspect can make poorly written C++ code harder to read and debug (see Aliasing).

However, because the operations on references are so limited, they are much easier to understand than pointers and are more resistant to errors. While pointers can be made invalid through a variety of mechanisms, ranging from carrying a null value to out-of-bounds arithmetic to illegal casts to producing them from random integers, a previously-valid reference only becomes invalid in two cases:

- If it refers to an object with automatic allocation which goes out of scope,
- If it refers to an object inside a block of dynamic memory which has been freed.

The first is easy to detect automatically if the reference has static scoping, but is still a problem if the reference is a member of a dynamically allocated object; the second is more difficult to assure. These are the only concern with references, and are suitably addressed by a reasonable allocation policy.

In addition, there are also *de facto* ways that a reference can start out invalid. Because a reference is usually implemented as an underlying pointer, initializing a reference on a pointer-dereferencing expression, will usually be implemented by the compiler as a simple assignment from the pointer to the underlying pointer of the reference. Thus, if you have a NULL pointer or a pointer pointing to an invalid location in memory, you will *de facto* have a reference that points to NULL or an invalid location. C++ purists would argue that, technically, dereferencing a NULL or invalid pointer leads to undefined behavior anyway, so this does not violate the assertions above that a reference cannot be null or point to arbitrary places in memory. However, this ignores the fact that in this case, the underlying implementation simply performs an "assignment", and there is no access of the memory location involved, so this initialization of the reference usually does not cause problems, and programmers must be aware of the possibility of a *de facto* "invalid" reference in a real program.

Analogies

- References can be thought of as "hard links" in file system terminology. Hard links can be modified as though they were the file they were linked to and when a hard link is deleted the original file remains. Similarly, references can be deleted (whether by going out of scope or explicitly being removed) and the original object that was referenced remains.

Source (edited): "http://en.wikipedia.org/wiki/Reference_(C%2B%2B)"

Return value optimization

Return value optimization, or simply **RVO**, is a C++-specific compiler optimization technique that involves eliminating the temporary object created to hold a function's return value. It is particularly notable for being allowed to change the observable behaviour of the resulting program.

Summary

In general, the C++ standard allows a compiler to perform any optimization, as long as the resulting executable exhibits the same observable behaviour *as if* all the requirements of the standard has been fulfilled. This is commonly referred to as the as-if rule. The term *return value optimization* refers to a special clause in the C++ standard that allows an implementation to omit a copy operation resulting from a return statement, even if the copy constructor has side effects, something that is not permitted by the *as-if rule* alone.

The following example demonstrates a scenario where the implementation may eliminate one or both of the copies being made, even if the copy constructor has a visible side effect (printing text). The first copy that may be eliminated is the one where C() is copied into the function f's return value. The second copy that may be eliminated is the copy of the temporary object returned by f to obj.

```
#include <iostream>

struct C
{
 C() {}
 C(const C&) { std::cout << "A copy
was made.\n"; }
};

C f()
{
 return C();
}

int main()
{
 std::cout << "Hello World!\n";
 C obj = f();
}
```

Depending upon the compiler, and that compiler's settings, the resulting program may display any of the following outputs:

```
Hello World!
A copy was made.
A copy was made.

Hello World!
A copy was made.

Hello World!
```

Background

Returning an object of builtin type from a function usually carries little to no overhead, since the object typically fits in a CPU register. Returning a larger object of class type may require more expensive copying from one memory location to another. To achieve this, an implementation may create a hidden object in the caller's stack frame, and pass the address of this object to the function. The function's return value is then copied into the hidden object. Thus, code such as this:

```
struct Data { char bytes[16]; };
Data f()
{
 Data result = {};
 // generate result
 return result;
}

int main()
{
 Data d = f();
}
```

May generate code equivalent to this:

```
struct Data { char bytes[16]; };

Data * f(Data * __hiddenAddress)
{
 Data result = {};
 // copy result into hidden object
 *__hiddenAddress = result;
 return __hiddenAddress;
}

int main()
{
 Data __hidden; // create hidden object
 Data d = *f(&__hidden); // copy the
result into d
}
```

which causes the Data object to be copied twice.

In the early stages of the evolution

of C++, the language's inability to efficiently return an object of class type from a function was considered a weakness. Around 1991, Walter Bright invented a technique to minimize copying, effectively replacing the hidden object and the named object inside the function with the object used to hold the result:

```
struct Data { char bytes[16]; };

void f(Data * p)
{
 // generate result directly in *p
}

int main()
{
 Data d;
 f(&d);
}
```

Bright implemented this optimization in his Zortech C++ compiler. This particular technique was later coined "Named return value optimization", referring to the fact that the copying of a named object is elided.

Compiler support

Return value optimization is supported on most compilers. There may be, however, circumstances where the compiler is unable to perform the optimization. One common case is when a function may return different named objects depending on the path of execution:

```
#include <string>
std::string f(bool cond = false)
{
 std::string first("first");
 std::string second("second");
 // the function may return one of two
named objects
 // depending on its argument. RVO
might not be applied
 if(cond)
  return first;
 else
  return second;
}

int main()
{
 std::string result = f();
}
```

Source (edited): "http://en.wikipedia.org/wiki/Return_value_optimization"

Rule of three (C++ programming)

The **rule of three** (also known as the Law of The Big Three or The Big Three) is a rule of thumb in C++ that claims that if a class defines one of the following it should probably explicitly define all three:

- destructor
- copy constructor
- copy assignment operator

These three functions are special member functions, if one of these functions is used without first being declared by the programmer it will be implicitly implemented by the compiler with the default semantics of doing the said operation on all the members of the class.

- **Destructor** - Destruct all the object's members
- **Copy constructor** - Construct all the object's members from the equivalent members in the copy constructor's parameter
- **Assignment operator** - Assign all the object's members from the equivalent members in the assignment operator's parameter

The Rule of Three claims that if one of these had to be defined by the programmer, it means that the compiler-generated version does not fit the needs of the class in one case and it will probably not fit in the other cases either. The term "Rule of three" was coined by Marshall Cline in 1991.

An amendment to this rule is that if Resource Acquisition Is Initialization (RAII) is used, the destructor may be left undefined (also known as The Law of The Big Two).

Because implicitly-generated constructors and assignment operators simply copy all class data members, one should define explicit copy constructors and copy assignment operators for classes that encapsulate complex data structures or have external references such as pointers, since only the pointer gets copied, not the object it points to.

Source (edited): "http://en.wikipedia.org/wiki/Rule_of_three_(C%2B%2B_programming)"

Run-time type information

In programming, **RTTI** (**Run-Time Type Information**, or **Run-Time Type Identification**) refers to a C++ system that makes information about an object's data type available at runtime. Run-time type information can apply to simple data types, such as integers and characters, or to generic objects. This is a C++ implementation of a more generic concept called reflection or, more specifically, type introspection.

In the original C++ design, Bjarne Stroustrup did not include run-time type information, because he thought this mechanism was frequently misused.

Features

The dynamic_cast<> operation and typeid operator in C++ are part of RTTI.

With C++ run-time type information, you can perform safe typecasts and manipulate type information at run time.

RTTI is available only for classes which are *polymorphic*, which means they have at least one virtual method. In practice, this is not a limitation because base classes must have a virtual destructor to allow objects of derived classes to perform proper cleanup if they are deleted from a base pointer.

RTTI is optional with some compilers—you choose at compile time whether to include the function. There may be a cost to making RTTI available even if the program does not use it.

C++ Example

```
/* A base class pointer can point to
objects of any class which is derived
 * from it. RTTI is useful to identify
which type (derived class) of object is
 * pointed to by a base cls pointer.
 */

#include <iostream>

class abc  // base class
{
public:
 virtual ~abc() { }
 virtual void hello()
 {
  std::cout << "in abc";
 }
};

class xyz : public abc
{
 public:
 void hello()
 {
  std::cout << "in xyz";
 }
};

int main()
{
 abc *abc_pointer = new xyz();
 xyz *xyz_pointer;

 // to find whether abc_pointer is
pointing to xyz type of object
 xyz_pointer = dynamic
_cast<xyz*>(abc_pointer);

 if (xyz_pointer != NULL)
 {
  std::cout << "abc_pointer is pointing
to a xyz class object";  // identified
 }
 else
 {
  std::cout << "abc_pointer is NOT
pointing to a xyz class object";
 }

 // needs virtual destructor
 delete abc_pointer;

 return 0;
}
```

An instance where RTTI is used is illustrated below:

```
class base {
  virtual ~base(){}
};

class derived : public base {
  public:
    virtual ~derived(){}
    int compare (derived &ref);
};

int my_comparison_method_for
_generic_sort (base &ref1, base &ref2)
{
  derived & d = dynamic_cast<derived
&>(ref1); // RTTI used here
  // RTTI enables the process to throw
a bad_cast exception
  // if the cast is not successful
  return d.compare (dynamic
_cast<derived &>(ref2));
}
```

Source (edited): "http://en.wikipedia.org/wiki/Run-time_type_information"

Scott Meyers

Scott Meyers is the author of three American books on the C++ computer programming language and a CD that integrates two of those books in electronic form. He is a frequent speaker at conferences and trade shows. He holds a Ph.D. in computer science from Brown University and M.S. in computer science from Stanford University.

Meyers is planning on writing a book titled *The Keyhole Problem*. The title refers to limitations on information visualization and human computer interaction caused by GUI elements that are not big enough to properly display their content, which can cause usability problems. These are *visible keyholes*. *Invisible keyholes* are caused by, for example, using too few bits to represent numbers, using signed vs. unsigned numbers, and restricted field sizes.

Among other points, Meyers has expressed opposition to asking programmers to solve design or programming problems during job interviews, making him a minority in this camp:

"I hate anything that asks me to design on the spot. That's asking to demonstrate a skill rarely required on the job in a high-stress environment, where it is difficult for a candidate to accurately prove their abilities. I think it's fundamentally an unfair thing to request of a candidate."

In March 2009, Meyers was awarded the Dr. Dobb's Journal Excellence in Programming Award.

Source (edited): "http://en.wikipedia.org/wiki/Scott_Meyers"

Seekg

In the C++ programming language, **seekg** is a function in the fstream library that allows you to seek to an arbitrary position in a file.

```
istream&  seekg ( streampos position );
istream&  seekg ( streamoff offset, ios
_base::seekdir dir );
```

- position is the new position in the stream buffer. This parameter is an object of type streampos.
- offset is and integer value of type streamoff representing the offset in the stream's buffer. It is relative to dir parameter.

dir is the seeking direction. It is an object of type ios_base::seekdir that can take any of the following constant values:

- ios_base::beg (offset from the beginning of the stream's buffer).
- ios_base::cur (offset from the current position in the stream's buffer).
- ios_base::end (offset from the end of the stream's buffer).

Note: If you have previously got an end of file on the stream, seekg will not reset it but will return an error in many implementations. - use the clear() method to clear the end of file bit first. This is a relatively common mistake and if seekg() is not performing as expected, it is wise to clear the fail bit, as shown below.

Example

```
#include <iostream>
#include <fstream>
using namespace std;

int main () {
  char buffer[10];

  fstream aFile; //input file
  aFile.open ("test.txt", ios::binary );
  aFile << "hello"; // inserts "hello"
into the file

  //seek to 3 characters from the
beginning of the file
  aFile.seekg (3, ios::beg);
  aFile.read (buffer,2); //read two
characters into the buffer
  buffer[3]=0; // end buffer with the
null terminating character
  aFile.close();

  cout << buffer << endl;
}
```

Example

```
#include <iostream>
#include <fstream>

int main () {
 string line;
 while (! myfile.eof())
 {
  /* this do-while loop continually
overwrites string "line" with the next
line from myfile
     until eof is reached. */
   getline(myfile,line);
 }

 // without this line, seekg() is
ineffective, as the fail bit is still there
 myfile.clear();

 myfile.seekg(0);
}
```

Source (edited): "http://en.wikipedia.org/wiki/Seekg"

Sequence point

A **sequence point** in imperative programming defines any point in a computer program's execution at which it is guaranteed that all side effects of previous evaluations will have been performed, and no side effects from subsequent evaluations have yet been performed. They are often mentioned in reference to C and C++, because the result of some expressions can depend on the order of evaluation of their subexpressions. Adding one or more sequence points is one method of ensuring a consistent result, because this restricts the possible orders of evaluation.

Examples of ambiguity

Consider two functions f() and g(). In C and C++, the + operator is not a sequence point, and therefore in the expression f()+g() it is possible that either f() or g() will be executed first. The comma operator is a sequence point, and therefore in the code f(),g() the order of evaluation is defined (i.e., first f() is called, and then g() is called). The type and value of the whole expression are those of g(); the value of f() is discarded.

Sequence points also come into play when the same variable is modified more than once within a single expression. An often-cited example is the expression i=i++, which both assigns i to itself and increments i. The final value of i is ambiguous, because, depending on the language semantics, the increment may occur before, after or interleaved with the assignment. The definition of a particular language might specify one of the possible behaviors or simply say the behavior is undefined. In C and C++, evaluating such an expression yields undefined behavior.

Sequence points in C and C++

In C and C++, sequence points occur in the following places. (In C++, overloaded operators act like functions, and thus operators that have been overloaded introduce sequence points in the same way as function calls.)

- Between evaluation of the left and right operands of the && (logical AND), || (logical OR), and comma operators. For example, in the expression *p++ != 0 && *q++ != 0, all side effects of the sub-expression *p++ != 0 are completed before any attempt to access q.
- Between the evaluation of the first operand of the ternary "question-mark" operator and the second or third operand. For example, in the expression a = (*p++) ? (*p++) : 0 there is a sequence point after the first *p++, meaning it has already been incremented by the time the second instance is executed.
- At the end of a full expression. This category includes expression statements (such as the assignment a=b;), return statements, the controlling expressions of if, switch, while, or do-while statements, and all three expressions in a for statement.
- Before a function is entered in a

function call. The order in which the arguments are evaluated is not specified, but this sequence point means that all of their side effects are complete before the function is entered. In the expression f(i++) + g(j++) + h(k++), f is called with a parameter of the original value of i, but i is incremented before entering the body of f. Similarly, j and k are updated before entering g and h respectively. However, it is not specified in which order f(), g(), h() are executed, nor in which order i, j, k are incremented. The values of j and k in the body of f are therefore undefined. Note that a function call f(a,b,c) is not a use of the comma operator and the order of evaluation for a, b, and c is unspecified.

- At a function return, after the return value is copied into the calling context. (This sequence point is only specified in the C++ standard; it is present only implicitly in C.)
- At the end of an initializer; for example, after the evaluation of 5 in the declaration int a = 5;.

Source (edited): "http://en.wikipedia.org/wiki/Sequence_point"

Significantly Prettier and Easier C++ Syntax

Significantly Prettier and Easier C++ Syntax or **SPECS** is an alternative syntactic binding for the semantics of C++.

Design

Designed by Ben Werther and Damian Conway, SPECS has a LALR(1) parsable grammar, which means it is significantly easier to parse than standard C++ syntax, both for computers and for humans alike. Also unlike standard C++ syntax, in SPECS declarations do not look like uses. For example, the fundamental C++ allocation control function set_new_handler has this declaration in orthodox C++ syntax:

```
void (*set_new_handler(void
(*)(void)))(void);
```

which in SPECS becomes:

```
func set_new_handler : ((void->void) -
> (void->void));
```

and using typedefs in C++:

```
typedef void (*new_handler)(void);
new_handler set_new_handler(new
_handler);
```

and in SPECS:

```
type new_handler : (void->void);
func set_new_handler : (new_handler -
> new_handler);
```

which in words can be described as function which both takes as an argument and returns, a pointer to a function that takes no arguments and returns void.

Apart from the declaration syntax change, the template syntax is changed to use <[ ]> brackets to make the template keyword unnecessary, several overloaded syntax elements are separated for clarity, := is used for assignment (instead of =), = is used for comparison (instead of ==), blocks for if-, for- and while-statements are mandatory, and there is no fallthrough for switch-statements.

Source (edited): "http://en.wikipedia.org/wiki/Significantly_Prettier_and_Easier_C%2B%2B_Syntax"

Single Compilation Unit

Single Compilation Unit is a C/C++ technique which reduces compilation time and aids the compiler to perform program optimization even when the compiler itself is lacking support for *whole program optimization* or precompiled headers.

Purpose

Usually a C/C++ development environment assumes that .c/.cpp source files are preprocessed (creating translation units) and translated separately by the compiler to object (.o or .obj) files, which can then be linked together to create an executable file or library. This leads to multiple passes being performed on common header files and, with C++, multiple template instantiations of the same templates in different translation units. The Single Compilation Unit technique uses pre-processor directives to "glue" different translation units together at compile-time, not link-time. This reduces the overall build time, but increases the build time required after making minor changes to any source file included in a Single Compilation Unit. So this technique is appropriate for some modules which consist of infrequently modified source files.

SCU also allows an optimizer to trace deeper relations between functions, therefore allowing optimizations such as inlining. It also helps avoiding implicit code bloat due to exceptions, side effects, and register allocation, which are generally overlooked by the classic scheme of using separate modules, and not always achieved by the use of precompiled headers.

Usage

For example, if you have the source files foo.cpp and bar.cpp, they can be placed in a Single Compilation Unit as follows:

```
#include "foo.cpp"
#include "bar.cpp"
```

Suppose foo.cpp and bar.cpp are:

```
//foo.cpp
#include <iostream> // A large,
```

```
standard header
#include "bar.cpp" // Declaration of function 'bar'

int main() // Definition of function 'main'
{
  bar();
}
```

```
//bar.cpp
#include <iostream> // The same large, standard header

void bar() // Definition of function 'bar'
{
  ...
}
```

Now the standard header file ('iostream') is compiled only once, and function 'bar' may be inlined into function 'main', despite being from another module.
Source (edited): "http://en.wikipedia.org/wiki/Single_Compilation_Unit"

sizeof

In the programming languages C and C++, the unary operator **sizeof** is used to calculate the sizes of datatypes, in number of bytes. A byte in this context is the same as an unsigned char, and may be larger than the standard 8 bits, although that is relatively uncommon in modern implementations. sizeof returns the size of the type of the variable or parenthesized type-specifier that it precedes as a size_t type value. sizeof can be applied to all datatypes, be they primitive types such as the integer and floating-point types defined in the language, pointers to memory addresses, or the compound datatypes (unions, structs, or C++ classes) defined by the programmer.

Need for sizeof

In many programs, there are situations where it is useful to know the size of a particular datatype (one of the most common examples is dynamic memory allocation using the library function malloc). Though for any given implementation of C or C++ the size of a particular datatype is constant, the sizes of even primitive types in C and C++ are implementation defined (that is, not precisely defined by the standard). This can cause problems when trying to allocate a block of memory of the appropriate size. For example, say a programmer wants to allocate a block of memory big enough to hold ten variables of type int. Because our hypothetical programmer doesn't know the exact size of type int, the programmer doesn't know how many bytes to ask malloc for. Therefore, it is necessary to use the operator sizeof:

```
/*pointer to type int, used to reference our allocated data*/
int * pointer = malloc(sizeof(int) * 10);
```

In the preceding code, the programmer instructs malloc to allocate and return a pointer to memory. The size of the block allocated is equal to the number of bytes a single object of type int takes up, multiplied by 10, ensuring enough space for all 10 ints.

It is generally not safe for a programmer to assume they know the size of any datatype. For example, even though most implementations of C and C++ on 32-bit systems define type int to be 4 bytes, it is recommended by many programmers to always use sizeof, as the size of an int could change when code is ported to a different system, breaking the code. In addition, it is frequently very difficult to predict the sizes of compound datatypes such as a struct or union due to structure "padding" (see Implementation below). Another reason for using sizeof is readability, as this avoids magic numbers.

Use

The sizeof operator is used to determine the amount of space any data-element/datatype occupies in memory. To use sizeof, the keyword "sizeof" is followed by a type name, variable, or expression. If a type name is used, it always needs to be enclosed in parentheses, whereas variable names and expressions can be specified with or without parentheses. A sizeof expression evaluates to an unsigned size_t value equal to the size in bytes of the "argument" datatype, variable, or expression (with datatypes, sizeof evaluates to the size of the datatype; for variables and expressions it evaluates to the size of the type of the variable or expression). For example, since sizeof(char) is defined to be 1 and assuming ints are 4 bytes long, the following code will print **1,4**:

```
/* the following code illustrates the use of sizeof
 * with variables and expressions (no parentheses needed),
 * and with type names (parentheses needed)
 */

char c;

printf("%zu,%zu\n", sizeof c, sizeof(int));
```

The value of a sizeof expression is always non-negative as the C standard specifies that the type of such an expression is size_t, defined to be an unsigned integer type. The z prefix should be used to print it, because the actual size can differ on each architecture.

Using sizeof with arrays

When sizeof is applied to an array, the result is the size in bytes of the array in memory. The following program uses sizeof to determine the size of an array, avoiding a buffer overflow when copying characters:

```
#include <stdio.h>
#include <string.h>

int main(int argc, char **argv)
{
  char buffer[10]; /* Array of 10 chars
*/

  /* Only copy 9 characters from argv
into buffer.
   * sizeof(char) is defined to be 1, so
the number of
   * elements in buffer is equal to its
size in bytes.
   */
  strncpy(buffer, argv[1], sizeof(buffer)
- sizeof(char));

  /* Set the last element of the buffer
equal to null */
  buffer[sizeof(buffer) - 1] = '\0';

  return 0;
}
```

Here, sizeof buffer is equivalent to 10*sizeof(char), or 10.

C99 adds support for flexible array members to structures. This form of array declaration is allowed as the last element in structures only, and differs from normal arrays in that no length is specified to the compiler:

```
#include <stdio.h>

struct flexarray
{
    char val;
    char array[];  /* Flexible array
member; must be last element of struct
*/
};

int main(int argc, char **argv)
{
    printf("sizeof(struct flexarray) = %
zu\n", sizeof(struct flexarray));

    return 0;
}
```

In this case the sizeof operator returns the size of the structure, including any padding, but without any storage allowed for the array. In the above example, the following output will be produced:

```
sizeof(struct flexarray) = 1
```

For structures containing flexible array members, sizeof is therefore equivalent to offsetof(s, array) where s is the structure name and array is the flexible array member.

C99 also allows variable length arrays where the length is specified at runtime . In such cases the sizeof operator is evaluated in part at runtime to determine the storage occupied by the array.

```
#include <stddef.h>
size_t flexsize(int n)
{
   char b[n+3];       /* Variable length
array */
   return sizeof b;  /* Execution time
sizeof */
}

int main()
{
  size_t size;
  size = flexsize(10); /* flexsize returns
13 */
  return 0;
}
```

sizeof and incomplete types

sizeof can only be applied to "completely" defined types. With arrays, this means that the dimensions of the array must be present in its declaration, and that the type of the elements must be completely defined. For structs and unions, this means that there must be a member list of completely defined types. For example, consider the following two source files:

```
/* file1.c */
int arr[10];
struct x {int one; int two;};
/* more code */

/* file2.c */
extern int arr[];
struct x;
/* more code */
```

Both files are perfectly legal C, and code in file1.c can apply sizeof to arr and struct x. However, it is illegal for code in file2.c to do this, because the definitions in file2.c are not complete. In the case of arr, the code does not specify the dimension of the array; without this information, the compiler has no way of knowing how many elements are in the array, and cannot calculate the array's overall size. Likewise, the compiler cannot calculate the size of struct x because it does not know what members it is made up of, and therefore cannot calculate the sum of the sizes of the structure's members. If the programmer provided the size of the array in its declaration in file2.c, or completed the definition of struct x by supplying a member list, this would allow him to apply sizeof to arr and struct x in that source file.

Implementation

It is the responsibility of the compiler's author to implement the sizeof operator in a way specific and correct for a given implementation of the language. The sizeof operator must take into account the implementation of the underlying memory allocation scheme to obtain the sizes of various datatypes. sizeof is usually a compile-time operator, which means that during compilation, sizeof and its operand get replaced by the result-value. This is evident in the assembly language code produced by a C or C++ compiler. For this reason, sizeof qualifies as an operator, even though its use sometimes looks like a function call. Applying sizeof to variable length arrays, introduced in C99, is an exception to this rule.

Structure padding

To calculate the sizes of user-defined types, the compiler takes into account any alignment space needed for complex user-defined data structures. This is why the size of a structure in C can be greater than the sum of the sizes of its members. For example, on many systems, the following code will print **8**:

```
struct student{
  char grade; /* char is 1 byte long */
  int age; /* int is 4 bytes long */
};

printf("%zu", sizeof (struct student));
```

The reason for this is that most compilers, by default, align complex data-structures to a word alignment boundary. In addition, the individual members are also aligned to their respective alignment boundaries. By this logic, the structure student gets aligned on a word boundary and the variable age within the structure is aligned with the next word address. This is accomplished by way of the compiler inserting "padding" space between two members or to the end of the structure to satisfy alignment requirements. This padding is inserted to align age with a word boundary. (Most processors can fetch an aligned word faster than they can fetch a word value that straddles multiple words in memory, and some don't support the operation at all).

Source (edited): "http://en.wikipedia.org/wiki/Sizeof"

Special member functions

Special member functions in C++ are functions which the compiler will automatically generate if they are used, but not declared explicitly by the programmer. The special member functions are:

- Default constructor (if no other constructor is explicitly declared)
- Copy constructor
- Copy assignment operator
- Destructor

In these cases the compiler generated versions of these functions perform a *memberwise* operation. For example the compiler generated destructor will destroy each sub-object (base class or member) of the object.

The compiler generated functions will be public, non-virtual and the copy constructor and assignment operators will receive const& parameters (and not be of the alternative legal forms).

Note: In C++0x with the introduction of move semantics, the move constructor and move assignment operator are added to the list of special member functions with the following rules.

- Both copy constructor and move constructor are defined by the compiler unless one of them was explicitly defined
- Both flavours of assignment operators are defined by the compiler unless one of them was explicitly defined

Example

The following example depicts two classes: Explicit for which all special member functions are explicitly declared and Implicit for which none are declared.

```
class Explicit {
   friend class Implicit;
   string msg;
   public:
    Explicit(void) : msg("")
    {
       cout << "Default constructor "
<< msg << endl;
    }
    Explicit(const string& value) :
msg(value)
    {
       cout << "Non-default constructor
" << msg << endl;
    }
    Explicit(const Explicit& other) :
msg(other.msg)
    {
       cout << "Copy constructor " <<
msg << endl;
    }
    Explicit& operator=(const Explicit
& other)
    {
       cout << "Copy assignment
operator " << msg << endl;
       if (this != &other)
       {
          msg = other.msg;
       }
       return *this;
    }
    ~Explicit(void)
    {
       cout << "Destructor " << msg <<
endl;
    }
};


class Implicit : public Explicit {
   int i;
   void* p;
   Explicit member;
   public:
    void Spew(void) { cout <<
"Implicit(" << msg << ", " << member.
msg << ")" << endl; };
};
```

In this case the class Implicit has not explicitly defined the destructor and the compiler will create a destructor equivalently to this:

```
// Sub-objects are destroyed in the
opposite order to their construction
Implicit::~Implicit()
{
   member.~Explicit(); // destroy
member
   (void)p;          // do nothing for p,
void* has no destructor
   (void)i;          // do nothing for i, int
has no destructor
   ~Explicit();      // call the base
class's destructor

}
```

Source (edited): "http://en.wikipedia.org/wiki/Special_member_functions"

string (C++)

In the C++ programming language, the std::**string** class is a standard representation for a string of text. This class removes many of the problems introduced by C-style strings by putting the onus of memory ownership on the string class rather than on the programmer. The class provides some typical string operations like comparison, concatenation, find and replace, and a function for obtaining substrings. It can be constructed from a C-style string, and a C-style string can also be obtained from it.

Usage

```
#include <iostream>
#include <string>

int main() {
  std::string foo = "hi";
  using std::string;
  // Now we can just say "string".
  string bar = "there";
  if (foo == bar) { // operator==
compares string contents for equality
    std::cout << "The strings are the
same"<<std::endl;// this line will not
print
  }
  std::cout << foo + bar << std::endl; //
Prints "hithere" (without quotes) by
creating a temporary object

  return 0;
}
```

Because a string may be stored by value, copying may take as long as $O(n)$ (i.e., copying takes time proportional to the length of the string). It will also cause heap memory to be allocated, which is usually far more expensive than the copy. For that reason, string is generally passed by reference-to-const to avoid unnecessary copying:

```
void print_the_string(const std::string
& str) {
  std::cout << str;
}
```

To interoperate with legacy code C-interfaces, it is often necessary to obtain a null-terminated string from a basic _string. The c_str() member function yields a pointer to the first element of an array whose elements correspond to the bytes in the original string and this array has a 0 at the offset of the length. If the null terminator is not needed, the data() method returns the pointer without any work needed to make sure the 0 is there. If the string is modified or its lifetime ends, the pointers returned by these methods become invalid.

Operators

The string class is fitted with a number of mathematical and logical operators for ease of use. All operators for the string class have member function equivalents, and all can accept another string or C string, so operators are purely for appearance and have no other advantage. All operators can also accept single characters; some libraries, however, might not accept a single character in the assignment operator (=). Most allow the left operand to be a C string.

The most basic, and obvious, is the assignment operator.

```
string str;
str = "abc"; // Assignment operator
accepts string literals.
str = 'a';  // Invalid in some libraries
//-- assignment operator might not
accept a char.
char* c_str1 = str; // Invalid -- a
character string
// cannot take the value of a string.
const char* c_str2 = str.c_str();  //
valid, but immutable;
//  do not delete c_str2!
char* c_str3 = new char[str.size() + 1];
strcpy(c_str3, str.c_str());
// mutable, but must delete c_str3
const char* c_str4 = str.data();
// similar to c_str(), but without
terminating zero byte
```

The + operator does concatenation.

```
string str1 = "qwe";
string str2 = "rty";

string str3;
str3 = str1 + str2;  // str3 = "qwerty"
str3 = "qwe" + str2; // Constructs a
temporary string object from the string
literal
str1 += str2; // str1 = "qwerty"

str1 -= str2; // Invalid -- subtraction
operations are not supported.
str3 = "qwe" + "rty"; // Invalid --
addition of string literals not defined
```

Strings can be tested for equality with operator==. This is a syntactic advantage to C-strings where operator== evaluates to true only if the pointers refer to the same address. Also, !=, <=, and >= are valid operations for strings. The following example assumes that the implementation uses ASCII character encoding.

```
string str1 = "Banana";
string str2 = "Banana";
string str3 = "banana";

assert( str1 == str2 );
assert( str1 != str3 );

string str4 = "Apple";
assert( str1 > str4 );
// True because 'A' is lower than 'B'
on the ASCII table.

assert( str1 < "apple" );
// True because 'B' comes before
lower-case 'a' on the ASCII table.
```

Lastly is the random access operator. It allows a string to act as an array of bytes, returning a reference to a char.

```
string person = "Jakw"; // Should be
"Jake".
person[3] = 'e';
char j = person[0];
```

The string class provides useful methods such as substr:

```
string str( "Apple Orange Banana" );
cout << "String at location 0 of length
5 is " << str.substr(0,5) << endl;
```

and find:

```
string str( "Apple Orange Banana" );
string::size_type loc = str.find(
"Orange", 0 );
if( loc != string::npos ) {
   cout << "Found Orange at " << loc
<< endl;
} else {
   cout << "Didn't find Orange" <<
endl;
}
```

Related classes

std::string is a typedef for a particular instantiation of the basic_string class template. Its definition is found in the <string> header and in the std namespace.

```
typedef basic_string<char> string;
```

which is equivalent to

```
basic_string<char, char_traits<char>,
allocator<char> >
```

Thus the class std::string provides functionality for strings consisting of the C char (not to be confused with actual "characters", which may consist of several of the units in the string, such as when UTF-8 encoding is used). There is a similar class std::wstring, which consists of wchar t, and is most often used to store UTF-16 text on Windows and UTF-32 on Unix. You can also make "strings" of any other object, even user-defined classes, similar to how you can make a std::vector of any class.
Source (edited): "http://en.wikipedia.org/wiki/String_(C%2B%2B)"

Substitution failure is not an error

Substitution failure is not an error (SFINAE) refers to a situation in C++ where an invalid substitution of template parameters is not in itself an error. David Vandevoorde first introduced the acronym SFINAE to describe related programming techniques.

Specifically, when creating a candidate set for overload resolution, some (or all) candidates of that set may be the result of substituting deduced template arguments for the template parameters. If an error occurs during substitution, the compiler removes the potential overload from the candidate set instead of stopping with a compilation error, provided the substitution error is one the C++ standard grants such treatment. If one or more candidates remain and overload resolution succeeds, the invocation is well-formed.

Example

The following example illustrates a basic instance of SFINAE:

```
struct Test
{
   typedef int type;
};

template < typename T >
void f(typename T::type) {} //
definition #1

template < typename T >
void f(T) {}              // definition #2

int main()
{
   f<Test>(10); // call #1
   f<int>(10);  // call #2 without error
thanks to SFINAE
}
```

Here, attempting to use a non-class type in a qualified name (T::type) results in a deduction failure for f<int> because int has no nested type named type, but the program is well-formed because a valid function remains in the set of candidate functions.

Although SFINAE was introduced to avoid creating ill-formed programs when unrelated template declarations were visible (e.g., through the inclusion of a header file), many developers found the behavior useful for compile-time introspection. Specifically, it allows a template to determine certain properties of its template arguments at instantiation time.

For example, SFINAE can be used to determine if a type contains a certain typedef:

```
#include <iostream>

template <typename T>
struct has_typedef_type
{
   // yes and no are guaranteed to have
different sizes,
   // specifically sizeof(yes) == 1 and
sizeof(no) == 2
   typedef char yes[1];
   typedef char no[2];

   template <typename C>
   static yes& test(typename C::type*);

   template <typename>
   static no& test(...);

   // if the sizeof the result of calling
test<T>(0) is equal to the sizeof(yes),
   // the first overload worked and T
has a nested type named type.
   static const bool value =
sizeof(test<T>(0)) == sizeof(yes);
};

struct foo
{
   typedef float type;
};

int main()
{
   std::cout << std::boolalpha;
   std::cout << has_typedef
_type<int>::value << std::endl;
   std::cout << has_typedef
_type<foo>::value << std::endl;
}
```

When T has the nested type type defined, the instantiation of the first test works and 0 is successfully passed as the null pointer constant. (And the resulting type of the expression is yes.) If it does not work, the only available function is the second test, and the resulting type of the expression is no. (An ellipsis is used not only because it will accept any argument, but also because its conversion rank is lowest, so a call to the first function will be preferred if it is possible; this removes ambiguity.)

Developers of Boost used SFINAE to great effect in boost::enable_if and in other ways.

Source (edited): "http://en.wikipedia.org/wiki/Substitution_failure_is_not_an_error"

Tech Edge

Tech Edge (Tech-Edge) is the annual computer fest organized by Birla Vidya Niketan as a part of their Cultural Fiesta "UTSAV". The fest lasts 1 day and usually takes place during July. THE event has various schools of DELHI participating to present their inventions.

Events

- Web Designing
- C++ Programming
- Multimedia Presentation
- Collage (Photoshop)

Events like gaming were held in the past but are now discontinued

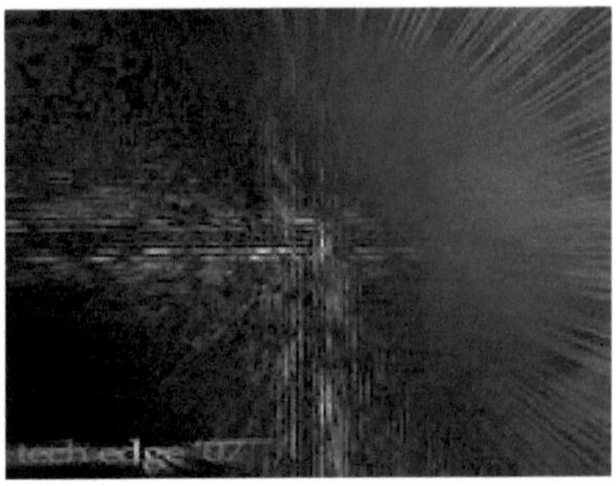

Tech Edge 2007 wallpaper

C++ Programming

Two rounds are held for this event. In the first round , the Prelims, each team comprising of 2 students is to clear an objective paper. The paper may also contain simple subjective questions. The top 10 teams to clear the prelims would compete in a 2 hour round. Some questions require intense thinking while others just require speed. Scoring is done taking into account the number of attempt calls, and the time taken.

Web Designing

Web Designing is held as a presentation event. Each team is to bring their pre-prepared websites on CDs and present their concept to the judges. The original files are also required to ensure that the work is their own.

Collage Making

One student from each school is to produce a collage from the images given to them. The topic is given on the spot and relevant images are provided. The software provided was Photoshop7.

Multimedia Presentation

In this event, the skills and creativity of students in forming multimedia presentations is tested. The students have to prepare a presentation in PowerPoint and also present it to the judges.

More information is available from the school.

Source (edited): "http://en.wikipedia.org/wiki/Tech_Edge"

Template (programming)

Templates are a feature of the C++ programming language that allow functions and classes to operate with generic types. This allows a function or class to work on many different data types without being rewritten for each one.

Templates are of great utility to programmers in C++, especially when combined with multiple inheritance and operator overloading. The C++ Standard Library provides many useful functions within a framework of connected templates.

Technical overview

There are two kinds of templates: *function templates* and *class templates*.

Function templates

A *function template* behaves like a function except that the template can have arguments of many different types (see example). In other words, a function template represents a family of functions. For example, the C++ Standard Library contains the function template max(x, y) which returns either *x* or *y*, whichever is larger. max() could be defined like this, using the following template:

```
#include <iostream>

template <typename T>
const T& max(const T& x, const T& y)
{
 if(y < x)
  return x;
 return y;
}
```

One definition of a function which works with different kinds of data types. A function template does not occupy space in memory. The actual definition of a function template is generated when the function is called with a specific data type. The function template does not save memory.

```
int main()
{
 // This will call max <int> (by argument deduction)
 std::cout << max(3, 7) << std::endl;
 // This will call max<double> (by argument deduction)
 std::cout << max(3.0, 7.0) << std::endl;
 // This type is ambiguous; explicitly instantiate max<double>
 std::cout << max<double>(3, 7.0) << std::endl;
 return 0;
}
```

In the first two cases, the template argument T is automatically deduced by the compiler to be int and double, respectively. In the third case deduction fails because the type of the parameters must in general match the template arguments exactly. This function template can be instantiated with any copy-constructible type for which the expression (y < x) is valid. For user-defined types, this implies that the less-than operator must be overloaded.

Class templates

A class template provides a specification for generating classes based on parameters. Class templates are commonly used to implement containers. A class template is instantiated by passing a given set of types to it as template arguments. The C++ Standard Library contains many class templates, in particular the containers adapted from the Standard Template Library, such as vector.

Explicit template specialization

When a function or class is instantiated from a template, a specialization of that template is created by the compiler for the set of arguments used (and the specialization is referred to as being a generated specialization). However, the programmer may decide to implement a special version of a function (or class) for a given set of template arguments which is called an explicit specialization. If a class template is specialized by a subset of its parameters it is called partial template specialization. If all of the parameters are specialized it is a *full specialization*. Function templates cannot be partially specialized.

Explicit specialization is used when the behavior of a function or class for particular choices of the template parameters must deviate from the generic behavior: that is, from the code generated by the main template, or templates.

Advantages and disadvantages

Some uses of templates, such as the maximum() function, were previously fulfilled by function-like preprocessor macros. For example, the following is a C++ maximum() macro:

```
#define maximum(a,b) ((a) < (b) ? (b)
: (a))
```

Both macros and templates are expanded at compile-time. Macros are always expanded inline, whereas templates are only expanded inline when the compiler deems it appropriate. When expanded inline, macro functions and template functions have no extraneous run-time overhead. Template functions with many lines of code will incur run-time overhead when they are not expanded inline, but the reduction in code size may help the code to load from disk more quickly and/or fit within RAM caches.

Templates are considered "type-safe", that is, they require type-checking at compile-time. Hence, the compiler can determine at compile-time whether or not the type associated with a template definition can perform all of the functions required by that template definition.

By design, templates can be utilized in very complex problem spaces, whereas macros are substantially more limited.

There are fundamental drawbacks to the use of templates:

- Historically, some compilers exhibited poor support for templates. So, the use of templates could decrease code portability.
- Many compilers lack clear instructions when they detect a template definition error. This can increase the effort of developing templates, and has prompted the development of Concepts for possible inclusion in a future C++ standard.
- Since the compiler generates additional code for each template type, indiscriminate use of templates can lead to code bloat, resulting in larger executables.
- Because a template by its nature exposes its implementation, injudicious use in large systems can lead to longer build times.
- It can be difficult to debug code that is developed using templates. Since the compiler replaces the templates, it becomes difficult for the debugger to locate the code at runtime.
- Templates of Templates (nesting) are not supported by all compilers, or might have a max nesting level.
- Templates are in the headers, which require a complete rebuild of all project pieces when changes are made.
- No information hiding. All code is exposed in the header file. No one library can solely contain the code.
- Virtual functions can cause excessive execution time bloat, and consume hundreds of kilobytes during run time space. (V Function Table).

Additionally, the use of the "less-than" and "greater-than" signs as delimiters is problematic for tools (such as text editors) which analyse source code syntactically. It is difficult, or maybe impossible, for such tools to determine whether a use of these tokens is as comparison operators or template delimiters. For example, this line of code:

```
foo (a < b, c > d) ;
```

may be a function call with two parameters, each the result of a comparison expression. Alternatively, it could be a declaration of a constructor for class foo taking one parameter, "d", whose type is the parametrised "a < b, c >".

Generic programming features in other languages

Initially, the concept of templates was not included in some languages, such as Java and C# 1.0. Java's adoption of generics mimics the behaviour of templates, but is technically different. C# added generics (parameterized types) in .NET 2.0. The generics in Ada predate C++ templates.

Although C++ templates, Java generics, and .NET generics are often considered similar, generics only mimic the basic behavior of C++ templates. Some of the advanced template features utilized by libraries such as Boost and STLSoft, and implementations of the STL itself, for template metaprogramming (explicit or partial specialization, default template arguments, template non-type arguments, template template arguments, ...) are not available with generics.

The D programming language attempts to build on C++ redesigning a better template system. A significant addition is the inclusion of the static if statement, which allows conditional compilation of code based on any information known at compile time. For example:

```
template Factorial(ulong n)
{
  static if( n <= 1 )
    const Factorial = 1;
  else
    const Factorial = n * Factorial!(n-
1);
};
```

Also note that the !() delimiters are used rather than the <> delimiters. This prevents ambiguity in the parsing of templates.

Other significant features include typesafe variadic template functions.

```
// Simple example, assumes all arguments are of the same type.
T[0] max(T...)(T args) {
    static assert(args.length > 1, "Insufficient arguments.");
    // T is the type of the first argument,
    // args is the first argument.
    T[0] max = args[0];
    // Tuple can be iterated over and sliced like an array.
    foreach (arg; args[1 .. $])
        if (arg > max)
            max = arg;
    return max;
}
```

This function will work for any number of arguments, with the foreach iteration over the tuple of arguments expanded at compile time.

D templates allow a simple form of Constraints too. They can be expressed as an arbitrarily complex predicate that must evaluate at compile time. If it's true the template is a match for the arguments, otherwise the template is ignored during overload matching.

```
template Foo(int N) if (N & 1)    {...} // A
template Foo(int N) if (!(N & 1)) {...} // B

Foo!(3)  // Instantiates A
Foo!(64) // Instantiates B

template Bar(T) if (isFloatingPoint!T) {...}

Bar!(3.5) // Instantiates Bar
Bar!(3)  // Fails
```

Something similar can be done in C++ with Boost enable_if.

In C++ templates, the compile-time cases are performed by pattern matching over the template arguments, so the Factorial template's base cases are implemented by matching 0 and 1 rather than with an inequality test, which is unavailable:

```
// Induction

template <int N> struct Factorial {
  static const int value = N * Factorial<N - 1>::value;
};

// Base cases via template specialization:

template <>
struct Factorial<0> {
  static const int value = 1;
};

template <>
struct Factorial<1> {
  static const int value = 1;
};
```

With these definitions, one can compute, say 6! at compile time using the expression Factorial<6>::value.
Source (edited): "http://en.wikipedia.org/wiki/Template_(programming)"

Template metaprogramming

Template metaprogramming is a metaprogramming technique in which templates are used by a compiler to generate temporary source code, which is merged by the compiler with the rest of the source code and then compiled. The output of these templates include compile-time constants, data structures, and complete functions. The use of templates can be thought of as compile-time execution. The technique is used by a number of languages, the best-known being C++, but also Curl, D, and XL.

Template metaprogramming was, in a sense, discovered accidentally: see History of TMP.

Some other languages support similar, if not more powerful compile-time facilities (such as Lisp macros), but those are outside the scope of this article.

Components of template metaprogramming

The use of templates as a metaprogramming technique requires two distinct operations: a template must be defined, and a defined template must be instantiated. The template definition describes the generic form of the generated source code, and the instantiation causes a specific set of source code to be generated from the generic form in the template.

Template metaprogramming is generally Turing-complete, meaning that any computation expressible by a computer program can be computed, in some form, by a template metaprogram.

Templates are different from *macros*. A macro, which is also a compile-time language feature, generates code in-line using text manipulation and substitution. Macro systems often have limited compile-time process flow abilities and usually lack awareness of the semantics and type system of their companion language (an exception should be made with Lisp's macros, which are written in Lisp, itself, and involve manipulation and substitution of Lisp code represented as data structures as opposed to text).

Template metaprograms have no mutable variables— that is, no variable can change value once it has been initialized, therefore template metaprogramming can be seen as a form of functional programming. In fact many template implementations only implement flow control through recursion, as seen in the example below.

Using template metaprogramming

Though the syntax of template metaprogramming is usually very different from the programming language it is used with, it has practical uses. Some common reasons to use templates are to implement generic programming (avoiding sections of code which are similar except for some minor variations) or to perform automatic compile-time optimization such as doing something once at compile time rather than every time the program is run — for instance, by having the compiler unroll loops to eliminate jumps and loop count decrements whenever the program is executed.

Compile-time class generation

What exactly "programming at compile-time" means can be illustrated with an example of a factorial function, which in non-template C++ can be written using recursion as follows:

```
unsigned int factorial(unsigned int n)
{
  if (n == 0)
    return 1;
  return n * factorial(n - 1);
}

void foo()
{
  int x = factorial(4); // == (4 * 3 * 2 *
1 * 1) == 24
  int y = factorial(0); // == 0! == 1
}
```

The code above will execute when the program is run to determine the factorial value of the literals 4 and 0.

Instead, by using template metaprogramming and template specialization to provide the ending condition for the recursion, the factorials used in the program, ignoring any factorial *not* used, can be calculated at compile-time by this code:

```
template <int N>
struct Factorial
{
  enum { value = N * Factorial<N -
1>::value };
};

template <>
struct Factorial<0>
{
  enum { value = 1 };
};

// Factorial<4>::value == 24
// Factorial<0>::value == 1
void foo()
{
  int x = Factorial<4>::value; // == 24
  int y = Factorial<0>::value; // == 1
}
```

The code above calculates the factorial value of the literals 4 and 0 at compile time and uses the result as if they were precalculated constants.

While the two versions are similar from the point of view of the program's functionality, the first example calculates the factorials at run time, while the second calculates them at compile time. However, to be able to use templates in this manner, the compiler must know the value of its parameters at compile time, which has the natural precondition that Factorial<*X*>::value can only be used if *X* is known at compile time. In other words, *X* must be a constant literal or a constant expression.

The difference between the two approaches is a conceptual one: optimizers may evaluate the first example's factorial(*X*) at compile time, too, if *X* is known at compile time. However, this kind of optimization is neither guaranteed nor achieved through programming, as it is in the case of template metaprogramming. The first example also has the effect of producing code of a function definition for computing factorials regardless of its being called or not, unlike the second example whose intention is to avoid producing a factorial function's code.

Compile-time code optimization

The factorial example above is one example of compile-time code optimization in that all factorials used by the program are pre-compiled and injected as numeric constants at compilation, saving both run-time overhead and memory footprint. It is, however, a relatively minor optimization.

As another, more significant, example of compile-time loop-unrolling, template metaprogramming can be used to create length-*n* vector classes (where *n* is known at compile time). The benefit over a more traditional length-*n* vector is that the loops can be unrolled, resulting in very optimized code. As an example, consider the addition operator. An length-*n* vector addition might be written as

```
template <int length>
Vector<length>&
Vector<length>::operator+=(const
Vector<length>& rhs)
{
  for (int i = 0; i < length; ++i)
    value[i] += rhs.value[i];
  return *this;
}
```

When the compiler instantiates the function template defined above, the following code may be produced:

```
template <>
Vector<2>& Vector<2>::operator+
=(const Vector<2>& rhs)
{
  value[0] += rhs.value[0];
  value[1] += rhs.value[1];
  return *this;
}
```

The compiler's optimizer should be able to unroll the for loop because the template parameter length is a constant at compile time.

However, take caution as this may cause code bloat as separate unrolled code will be generated for each 'N'(vector size) you instantiate with.

Static polymorphism

Polymorphism is a common standard programming facility where derived objects can be used as instances of their base object but where the derived objects' methods will be invoked, as in this code

```
class Base
{
public:
   virtual void method() { std::cout << "Base"; }
   virtual ~Base() {}
};

class Derived : public Base
{
public:
   virtual void method() { std::cout << "Derived"; }
};

int main()
{
   Base *pBase = new Derived;
   pBase->method(); //outputs "Derived"
   delete pBase;
   return 0;
}
```

where all invocations of virtual methods will be those of the most-derived class. This *dynamically polymorphic* behaviour is (typically) obtained by the creation of virtual look-up tables for classes with virtual methods, tables that are traversed at run time to identify the method to be invoked. Thus, *run-time polymorphism* necessarily entails execution overhead (though on modern architectures the overhead is negligible).

However, in many cases the polymorphic behaviour needed is invariant and can be determined at compile time. Then the Curiously Recurring Template Pattern (CRTP) can be used to achieve *static polymorphism*, which is an imitation of polymorphism in programming code but which is resolved at compile time and thus does away with run-time virtual-table lookups. For example:

```
template <class Derived>
struct base
{
   void interface()
   {
      // ...
      static_cast<Derived*>(this)->implementation();
      // ...
   }
};

struct derived : base<derived>
{
    void implementation();
};
```

Here the base class template will take advantage of the fact that member function bodies are not instantiated until after their declarations, and it will use members of the derived class within its own member functions, via the use of a static_cast, thus at compilation generating an object composition with polymorphic characteristics. As an example of real-world usage, the CRTP is used in the Boost iterator library .

Another similar use is the "Barton–Nackman trick", sometimes referred to as "restricted template expansion", where common functionality can be placed in a base class that is used not as a contract but as a necessary component to enforce conformant behaviour while minimising code redundancy.

Benefits and drawbacks of template metaprogramming

- **Compile-time versus execution-time tradeoff**: If a great deal of template metaprogramming is used, compilation may become slow; section 14.7.1 [temp.inst] of the current standard defines the circumstances under which templates are implicitly instantiated. As with most aspects of C++, you pay only for what you use: defining a template does not imply that it will be instantiated, and instantiating a class template does not cause its member definitions to be instantiated. Depending on the style of use, templates may compile either faster or slower than hand-rolled code.
- **Generic programming**: Template metaprogramming allows the programmer to focus on architecture and delegate to the compiler the generation of any implementation required by client code. Thus, template metaprogramming can accomplish truly generic code, facilitating code minimization and better maintainability.
- **Readability**: With respect to C++, the syntax and idioms of template metaprogramming are esoteric compared to conventional C++ programming, and advanced template metaprogramming (or even the simplest non-trivial template metaprogramming) can be very difficult to understand. Metaprograms can thus be difficult to maintain by programmers inexperienced in template metaprogramming (though this may vary with the language's implementation of template metaprogramming syntax). On the other hand, template metaprogramming can often be used to make programs much shorter and simple, and thus more readable. An experienced programmer will also be able to tweak the program and use the compiler error messages to understand the program flow much more easily that could have been achieved by any non-metaprogramming approach.
- **Portability**: With respect to C++, due to differences in compilers, code relying heavily on template metaprogramming (especially the newest forms of metaprogramming) might have portability issues.

Source (edited): "http://en.wikipedia.org/wiki/Template_metaprogramming"

The lexer hack

When parsing computer programming languages, **the lexer hack** (as opposed to "a lexer hack") describes a common solution to the problems which arise when attempting to use a regular grammar-based lexer to classify tokens in ANSI C as either variable names or type names.

Problem

In a compiler, the lexer performs one of the earliest stages of converting the source code to a program. It scans the text to extract meaningful *tokens*, such as words, numbers, and strings. The parser analyzes sequences of tokens attempting to match them to syntax rules representing language structures, such as loops and variable declarations. A problem occurs here if a single sequence of tokens can ambiguously match more than one syntax rule.

This ambiguity can happen in C if the lexer does not distinguish between variable and typedef identifiers. For example, in the C expression:

```
(A) * B
```

the lexer may find these tokens:

- left parenthesis
- identifier 'A'
- right parenthesis
- operator '*'
- identifier 'B'

The parser can interpret this as variable *A* multiplied by *B* or as type *A* casting the dereferenced value of *B*. This is known as the "typedef-name: identifier" problem.

The hack solution

The solution generally consists of feeding information from the parser's symbol table back into the lexer. This incestuous mixing of the lexer and parser is generally regarded as inelegant, which is why it is called a "hack". The lexer cannot distinguish type identifiers from other identifiers without extra context because all identifiers have the same format.

With the hack in the above example, when the lexer finds the identifier *A* it should be able to classify the token as a type identifier. The rules of the language would be clarified by specifying that typecasts require a type identifier and the ambiguity disappears.

The problem also exists in C++ and parsers can use the same hack.

Alternative solutions

This problem does not arise (and hence needs no "hack" in order to solve) when using lexerless parsing techniques.

Some parser generators, such as the yacc-derived BtYacc ("Backtracking Yacc"), give the generated parser the ability to try multiple attempts to parse the tokens. In the problem described here, if an attempt fails because of semantic information about the identifier, it can backtrack and attempt other rules.
Source (edited): "http://en.wikipedia.org/wiki/The_lexer_hack"

Traits class

In computer programming, a **traits class** is a class template used to associate information or behaviour to a compile-time entity, typically a data type or a constant, without modifying the existing entity. In the C++ programming language, this is normally achieved by defining a primary class template, and creating explicit or partial specializations for the relevant types.

Usage

It is used in Standard Template Library and the C++ standard library to support generic container classes. The technique is used extensively in the Boost TypeTraits library.
Source (edited): "http://en.wikipedia.org/wiki/Traits_class"

typedef

typedef is a keyword in the C and C++ programming languages. The purpose of typedef is to assign alternative names to existing types, most often those whose standard declaration is cumbersome, potentially confusing, or likely to vary from one implementation to another.

Under C convention (such as in the C standard library), types declared with typedef end with '_t' (e.g., size_t, time_t).

Usage examples

Indicating what a variable represents

A typedef can be used to indicate how a variable represents something, e.g., units of measurement or counts:

```
int current_speed ;
int high_score ;
...

void congratulate(int your_score) {
  if (your_score > high_score)
...
```

Now consider this:

```
typedef int km_per_hour ;
typedef int points ;

km_per_hour current_speed ;
points high_score ;
...

void congratulate(points your_score) {
  if (your_score > high_score)
...
```

Both sections of code do the same thing. However, the use of typedef in the second example makes it clear that the two variables, while represented by the same data type (int), represent different and incompatible things. The declaration in congratulate() of your_score indicates to the programmer that current _speed (or any other variable not declared as a points) should not be passed as an argument. This would not be as apparent if both were declared as ints. However, note that the indication is *for the programmer only*; the C/C++ compiler considers both variables to be ints, and will not give any type mismatch warnings or errors if current_speed is used as the argument for a call to congratulate().

Simplifying a declaration

A typedef can be used to simplify the declaration for a compound type (struct, union) or pointer type such as:

```
struct var {
   int data1;
   char data2;
};
```

Here (above) a *struct var* data type has been defined. To declare a variable of this type in C the struct key word is required (though it can be omitted in C++):

```
struct var a;
```

A typedef can be used to eliminate the need for the struct key word in C. For example, with:

```
typedef struct var newtype;
```

we can now create a variable of this type with:

```
newtype a;
```

Note that the structure definition and typedef can instead be combined into a single statement:

```
typedef struct var {
   int data1;
   char data2;
} newtype;
```

Or simply we can also use it as:

```
typedef struct {
   int data1;
   char data2;
} newtype;
```

In C++, in contrast to C, the struct, class, and enum key words are optional in variable declarations that are separate from the definitions:

```
struct var x;      // This is legal
var y;             // This is also legal
```

As such, var can be used wherever newtype can be used. However, the reverse is not true; for instance, the constructor methods for var cannot be named newtype.

Using typedef with pointers

Typedefs can also simplify declarations for pointer types. Consider this:

```
struct Node {
   int data;
   struct Node *nextptr;
};
```

In C, one can declare multiple variables of the same type in a single statement, even mixing pointer and non-pointers. However, one would need to prefix an asterisk to each variable to assign it a pointer:

```
struct Node *startptr, *endptr, *curptr,
*prevptr, errptr, *refptr;
```

A programmer would assume that errptr was indeed a Node *, but a typographical error means that errptr is a Node. This can lead to subtle syntax errors.

By defining a Node * typedef, it is assured that all the variables will be pointer types.

```
typedef struct Node *NodePtr;
...
NodePtr startptr, endptr, curptr,
prevptr, errptr, refptr;
```

Using typedef with type casts

A typedef is created using type *declaration* syntax but can be used as if it were created using type *cast* syntax. For instance, in each line after the first line of:

```
typedef int (*funcptr)(double);      //
pointer to function of double returning
int
funcptr x = (funcptr) NULL;          //
C or C++
funcptr y = funcptr(NULL);           //
C or C++
funcptr z = static
_cast<funcptr>(NULL); // C++ only
```

funcptr is used on the left-hand side to declare a variable and is used on the right-hand side to cast a value. Thus, typedefs can be used by programmers who do not wish to figure out how to convert declaration syntax to type cast syntax.

Note that, without the typedef, it is generally not possible to use declaration syntax and cast syntax interchangeably. For example:

```
void *p = NULL;
int (*x)(double)  = (int (*)(double)) p;
// This is legal
int (*)(double) y = (int (*)(double)) p;
// Left-hand side is not legal
int (*z)(double)  = (int (*p)(double));
// Right-hand side is not legal
```

Usage concerns

Some people are opposed to the extensive use of typedefs. Most arguments center on the idea that typedefs simply hide the actual data type of a variable. For example, Greg Kroah-Hartman, a Linux kernel hacker and documenter, discourages their use for anything except function prototype declarations. He argues that this practice not only unnecessarily obfuscates code, it can also cause programmers to accidentally misuse large structures thinking them to be simple types.

Others argue that the use of typedefs can make code easier to maintain. K&R states that there are two reasons for using a typedef. First, it provides a means to make a program more portable. Instead of having to change a type everywhere it appears throughout the program's source files, only a single typedef statement needs to be changed. Second, a typedef can make a complex declaration easier to understand.

Usage in C++

In C++ type names can be very complicated and typedef provides a mechanism to assign a simple name to the type. Consider:

```
std::vector<std::pair<std::string, int> > values;
for (std::vector<std::pair<std::string, int> >::const_iterator i = values.begin(); i != values.end(); ++i)
{
  std::pair<std::string, int> const & t = *i;
  // do something
}
```

and

```
typedef std::pair<std::string, int> value_t;
typedef std::vector<value_t> values_t;

values_t values;
for (values_t::const_iterator i = values.begin(); i != values.end(); ++i)
{
  value_t const & t = *i;
  // do something
}
```

Use with C++ templates

There is no direct way to have templated typedefs in C++. For instance, to have value_t<T> represent std::pair<std::string, T> for every class T one *cannot* use:

```
template<class T>
typedef std::pair<std::string, T> value_t<T>; // Doesn't work
```

However, if one is willing to accept value_t<T>::foo, or similar, in lieu of value_t<T> then it is possible to achieve the desired result via a typedef within a templated class or structure:

```
template<class T>
struct value_t
{
  // Make value_t<T>::foo represent std::pair<std::string, T>
  typedef std::pair<std::string, T> foo;
};
```

Other languages

In many statically-typed functional languages, like Haskell, Miranda, OCaml, etc., you can define *type synonyms*, which are the same as typedefs in C. An example in Haskell:

```
type PairOfInts = (Int, Int)
```

This example has defined a type synonym "PairOfInts" which means the same as a pair of Ints.

C# also contains a feature which is similar to the typedef of C; however, it must be redeclared for each separate file. See this MSDN article for more

```
using newType = global::System.Runtime.Interop.Marshal;
using otherType = Enums.MyEnumType;
```

Source (edited): "http://en.wikipedia.org/wiki/Typedef"

typeid

In C++, the **typeid** keyword is used to determine the class of an object at runtime. It returns a reference to std::type_info object, which exists until the end of the program. The use of typeid is often preferred over dynamic_cast<*class_type*> in situations where just the class information is needed, because typeid, applied on a type or non de-referenced value is a constant-time procedure, whereas dynamic_cast must traverse the class derivation lattice of its argument at runtime. However, you should not rely on the exact content, such as that returned by std::type_info::name(), as this is implementation specific with respect to the compiler.

Objects of class std::bad_typeid are thrown when typeid is called on a dereferenced null pointer. The class is derived from std::exception, and thrown by typeid and others.

It is generally only useful to use typeid on the dereference of a pointer or reference (i.e. typeid(*ptr) or typeid(ref)) to an object of polymorphic class type (a class with at least one virtual function) because these are the only expressions that are associated with run-time type information. The type of any other expression is known at compile time.

Example

```
#include <iostream>
#include <typeinfo> //for 'typeid' to work

class Person {
public:
  // ... Person members ...
  virtual ~Person() {}
};

class Employee : public Person {
  // ... Employee members ...
};

int main ()
{
  Person person;
  Employee employee;
  Person *ptr = &employee;
  Person &ref = employee;
  // The string returned by typeid::name is implementation-defined
  std::cout << typeid(person).name() << std::endl;  // Person (statically known at compile-time)
  std::cout << typeid(employee).name() << std::endl; // Employee (statically known at compile-time)
  std::cout << typeid(ptr).name() << std::endl;     // Person * (statically known at compile-time)
  std::cout << typeid(*ptr).name() << std::endl;    // Employee (looked up dynamically at run-time

//          because it is the dereference of a

//          pointer to a polymorphic class)
  std::cout << typeid(ref).name() << std::endl;     // Employee (references can also be polymorphic)
}
```

Output (exact output varies by system):

```
Person
Employee
Person*
Employee
Employee
```

Source (edited): "http://en.wikipedia.org/wiki/Typeid"

typename

"**typename**" is a keyword in the C++ programming language with two distinct uses related to templates. It is a synonym for "class" in template parameters, and it is used to specify that a dependent name in a template definition or declaration is a type.

A synonym for "class"

In C++'s generic programming feature known as "templates", typename can be used to introduce a template parameter:

```
// Define a generic function that returns the greater of its two arguments
template <typename T>
const T& max(const T& x, const T& y)
{
  if (y < x)
    return x;
  return y;
}
```

An alternative and semantically equivalent keyword in this scenario is "class":

```
// Define a generic function that returns the greater of its two arguments
template <class T>
const T& max(const T& x, const T& y)
{
  if (y < x)
    return x;
  return y;
}
```

A method for indicating that a dependent name is a type

Consider this invalid code:

```
template <typename T>
void foo(const T& t)
{
  // declare a pointer to an object of type T::bar
  T::bar * p;
}

struct StructWithBarAsType {
  typedef int bar;
};

int main() {
  StructWithBarAsType x;
  foo(x);
}
```

This code looks like it should compile, but it is incorrect because the compiler does not know if T::bar is a type or a value. The reason it doesn't know is that T::bar is a "template-parameter dependent name", or "dependent name" for short, and as such could represent anything named "bar" inside a type passed to foo(), which could include typedefs, enums, variables, etc.

To resolve this ambiguity, the C++ Language Standard declares:

A name used in a template declaration or definition and that is dependent on a template-parameter is assumed not to name a type unless the applicable name lookup finds a type name or the name is qualified by the keyword typename.

In short, if the compiler can't tell if a dependent name is a value or a type, then it will assume that it is a value.

In our example, where T::bar is the dependent name, that means that rather than declaring a pointer to T::bar named "p", the line

```
T::bar * p;
```

will instead multiply the "value" T::bar times p (which is nowhere to be found) and throw away the result. The fact that in StructWithBarAsType the dependent bar is in fact a type does not help since foo() could be compiled long before StructWithBarAsType is seen. Furthermore, if there is also a class like:

```
struct StructWithBarAsValue {
    int bar;
};
```

then the compiler would be obliged to interpret the same template function in completely different ways.

The solution to this problem is to explicitly tell the compiler that T::bar is in fact a type. For this, the typename keyword is used:

```
template <typename T>
void foo(const T& t)
{
  // declare a pointer to an object of type T::bar
  typename T::bar * p;
}
```

Now the compiler knows for sure that T::bar is a type, and will correctly make p a pointer to an object of that type.

Source (edited): "http://en.wikipedia.org/wiki/Typename"

Undefined behavior

In computer programming, **undefined behavior** is a feature of some programming languages — most famously C. In these languages, to simplify the specification and allow some flexibility in implementation, the specification leaves the results of certain operations specifically *undefined*.

For example, in C the use of any automatic variable before it has been initialized yields undefined behavior, as do division by zero and indexing an array outside of its defined bounds (see buffer overflow). This specifically frees the compiler to do whatever is easiest or most efficient, should such a program be submitted. In general, any behavior afterwards is also undefined. In particular, it is never required that the compiler diagnose undefined behavior — therefore, programs invoking undefined behavior may appear to compile and even run without errors at first, only to fail on another system, or even on another date. When an instance of undefined behavior occurs, so far as the language specification is concerned *anything could happen*, maybe nothing at all.

Under some circumstances there can be specific restrictions on undefined behavior. For example, the instruction set specifications of a CPU might leave the behavior of some forms of an instruction undefined, but if the CPU supports memory protection then the specification will probably include a blanket rule stating that no user-accessible instruction may cause a hole in the operating system's security; so an actual CPU would be permitted to corrupt any or all user registers in response to such an instruction but would not be allowed to, for example, switch into supervisor mode.

Examples in C

Attempting to modify a string literal causes undefined behavior:

```
void f(void)
{
 char * p = "wikipedia"; // in C++, this requires deprecated implicit conversion from const char[] to char*
 p[0] = 'W'; // undefined behaviour
}
```

Division by zero results in undefined behavior:

```
int f(int x)
{
 return x/0; // undefined behavior
}
```

Certain pointer operations may result in undefined behavior:

```
void f(void)
{
 int arr[4] = {0, 1, 2, 3};
 int * p = arr + 5; // undefined behavior
}
```

The C Programming Language written by Kernighan and Ritchie cites the following examples of code that have undefined behavior in Section 2.12.

```
printf("%d %d\n", ++n, power(2, n));
/* WRONG */
```

and

```
a[i] = i++;
```

Risks of undefined behavior

HTML versions 4 and earlier left error handling undefined. Over time pages started relying on unspecified error-recovery implemented in popular browsers. This caused difficulties for vendors of less-popular browsers who were forced to reverse-engineer and implement bug compatible error recovery. This has led to de-facto standard that was much more complicated than it could have been if this behavior was specified from the start.

Compiler easter eggs

In some languages (including C), even the *compiler* is not bound to behave in a sensible manner once undefined behavior has been invoked. One instance of undefined behavior acting as an Easter egg is the behavior of early versions of the GCC C compiler when given a program containing the #pragma directive, which has implementation-defined behavior according to the C standard. ("Implementation-defined" is more restrictive than "undefined", requiring the implementation to document what it does.) In practice, many C implementations recognize, for example, #pragma once as a rough equivalent of #include guards — but GCC 1.21, upon finding a #pragma directive, would instead attempt to launch commonly distributed Unix games such as *NetHack* and *Rogue*, or start Emacs running a simulation of the Towers of Hanoi.

Source (edited): "http://en.wikipedia.org/wiki/Undefined_behavior"

Variadic macro

A **variadic macro** is a feature of the C preprocessor whereby a macro may be declared to accept a varying number of arguments.

Variable-argument macros were introduced in the **ISO/IEC 9899:1999** (C99) revision of the C programming language standard in 1999. They are currently *not* part of the C++ programming language, though many popular C++ implementations support variable-argument macros as an extension, and it is expected that variadic macros may be added to C++ at a later date.

Declaration syntax

The declaration syntax is similar to that of variadic functions: an *ellipsis* "..." is used to indicate that zero or more arguments must be passed. During macro expansion each occurrence of the special identifier __VA_ARGS__ in the macro replacement list is replaced by the passed arguments. The macro processor prevents dangling commas that might otherwise occur when zero arguments are substituted.

No means is provided to access individual arguments in the variable argument list, nor to find out how many were passed. However, macros can be written to count the number of arguments that have been passed.

Support

The GNU Compiler Collection, since 3.0, C++Builder 2006 and Visual Studio 2005 support variable-argument macros, both when compiling C and C++ code. In addition, GCC supports variadic macros when compiling Objective-C. Sun Studio C and C++ have had support since Forte Developer 6 update 2 (C++ version 5.3).

Example

If a printf-like function dprintf() were desired, which would take the file and line number from which it was called as arguments, the following macro might be used:

```
void realdprintf (char const *file, int line, ...);
#define dprintf(...) realdprintf(__FILE__, __LINE__, __VA_ARGS__)
```

dprintf() could then be called as:

```
dprintf("Hello, world");
```

which expands to:

realdprintf(__FILE__, __LINE__, "Hello, world");

or:

dprintf("%d + %d = %d", 2, 2, 5);

which expands to:

realdprintf(__FILE__, __LINE__, "%d + %d = %d", 2, 2, 5);

Without variadic macros, writing wrappers to printf is not directly possible. The standard workaround is to use the stdargs functionality of C/C++, and have the function call vprintf instead.

Source (edited): "http://en.wikipedia.org/wiki/Variadic_macro"

Virtual function

In object-oriented programming, a **virtual function** or **virtual method** is a function or method whose behaviour can be overridden within an inheriting class by a function with the same signature. This concept is a very important part of the polymorphism portion of object-oriented programming (OOP).

Purpose

The concept of the virtual function solves the following problem:

In OOP when a derived class inherits a base class, an object of the derived class may be referred to (or cast) as either being the base class type or the derived class type. If there are base class methods overridden by the derived class, the method call behaviour is ambiguous.

The distinction between virtual and non-virtual resolves this ambiguity. If the function in question is designated "virtual" in the base class then the derived class's function would be called (if it exists). If it is not virtual, the base class's function would be called.

Virtual functions overcome the problems with the type-field solution by allowing the programmer to declare functions in a base class that can be redefined in each derived class.

In C++ *virtual functions* or *virtual methods* are declared by using the *virtual* keyword to the function's declaration.

Example

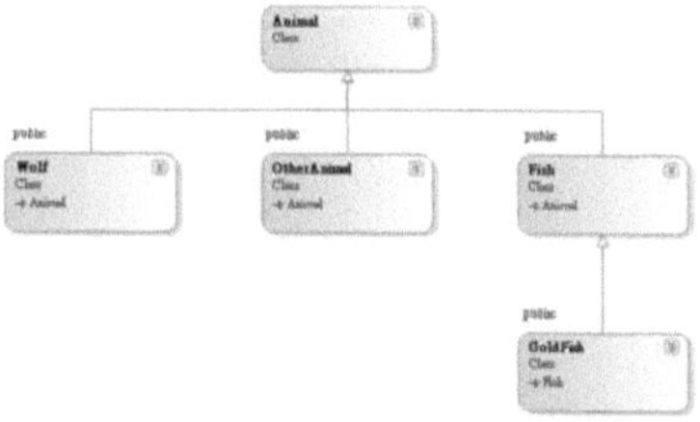

Class Diagram of Animal

For example, a base class Animal could have a virtual function eat. Subclass Fish would implement eat() differently than subclass Wolf, but you can invoke eat() on any class instance referred to as Animal, and get the eat() behaviour of the specific subclass.

This allows a programmer to process a list of objects of class Animal, telling each in turn to eat (by calling eat()), with no knowledge of what kind of animal may be in the list. You also do not need to have knowledge of how each animal eats, or what the complete set of possible animal types might be.

C++

The following is an example in C++. Note that this example is not exception-safe. In particular, it may leak resources if new or vector::push_back throws an exception.

```
#include <iostream>
#include <vector>

class Animal {
  public:
    virtual void eat() const {
      std::cout << "I eat like a
generic Animal." << std::endl;
    }
    virtual ~Animal() {
    }
};

class Wolf : public Animal {
  public:
    void eat() const {
      std::cout << "I eat like a wolf!"
<< std::endl;
    }
    virtual ~Wolf() {
    }
};

class Fish : public Animal {
  public:
    void eat() const {
      std::cout << "I eat like a fish!"
<< std::endl;
    }
    virtual ~Fish() {
    }
};

class GoldFish : public Fish {
  public:
    void eat() const {
      std::cout << "I eat like a
goldfish!" << std::endl;
    }
    virtual ~GoldFish() {
    }
};

class OtherAnimal : public Animal {
    virtual ~OtherAnimal() {
    }
};

int main() {
  std::vector<Animal*> animals;
  animals.push_back(new Animal());
  animals.push_back(new Wolf());
  animals.push_back(new Fish());
  animals.push_back(new GoldFish());
  animals.push_back(new
OtherAnimal());

  for (std::vector<Animal*>::const
_iterator it = animals.begin(); it !=
animals.end(); ++it) {
    (*it)->eat();
    delete *it;
  }

  return 0;
}
```

Output with the virtual function Animal::eat():

```
I eat like a generic Animal.
I eat like a wolf!
I eat like a fish!
I eat like a goldfish!
I eat like a generic Animal.
```

Output if Animal::eat() were not declared as virtual:

```
I eat like a generic Animal.
I eat like a generic Animal.
I eat like a generic Animal.
I eat like a generic Animal.
I eat like a generic Animal.
```

D

The D programming language implements virtual functions. The "override" keyword tells the compiler that we don't want to define a new function, but rather override an existing one. Thus if no function with the same name exists in the base class, the compiler breaks with an error. Note that the example below would produce the same output without the override keyword, but would also throw a compilation warning: *Error: overrides base class function test.main.Animal.eat, but is not marked with 'override'.*

```
import std.stdio;

void main()
{
    class Animal
    {
        void eat() { writefln("I eat
like a generic Animal."); }
    }

    class Wolf : Animal
    {
        override void eat() {
writefln("I eat like a Wolf."); }
    }

    class Fish : Animal
    {
        override void eat() {
writefln("I eat like a Fish."); }
    }

    class GoldFish : Fish
    {
        override void eat() {
writefln("I eat like a GoldFish."); }
    }

    class OtherAnimal : Animal
    {
    }

    Animal[] animals = new
Animal[5];
    animals[0] = new Animal;
    animals[1] = new Wolf;
    animals[2] = new Fish;
    animals[3] = new GoldFish;
    animals[4] = new OtherAnimal;

    foreach ( Animal a; animals)
        a.eat();
}
```

Output:

```
I eat like a generic Animal.
I eat like a wolf!
I eat like a fish!
I eat like a goldfish!
I eat like a generic Animal.
```

Java

In Java, all non-static methods are by default "virtual functions." Only methods marked with the keyword final, which cannot be overridden, along with private methods, which are not inherited, are non-virtual. The following is an example of virtual methods in Java:

```
import java.util.*;

public class Animal
{
  public void eat()
  {
    System.out.println("I eat like a
generic Animal.");
  }

  public static void main(String[] args)
  {
    List<Animal> animals = new
LinkedList<Animal>();

    animals.add(new Animal());
    animals.add(new Wolf());
    animals.add(new Fish());
    animals.add(new Goldfish());
    animals.add(new OtherAnimal());

    for (Animal currentAnimal :
animals)
    {
      currentAnimal.eat();
    }
  }
}

public class Wolf extends Animal
{
  @Override
  public void eat()
  {
    System.out.println("I eat like a
wolf!");
  }
}

public class Fish extends Animal
{
  @Override
  public void eat()
  {
    System.out.println("I eat like a
fish!");
  }
}

public class Goldfish extends Fish
{
  @Override
  public void eat()
  {
    System.out.println("I eat like a
goldfish!");
  }
}

public class OtherAnimal extends
Animal {}
```

Output:

```
I eat like a generic Animal.
I eat like a wolf!
I eat like a fish!
I eat like a goldfish!
I eat like a generic Animal.
```

Delphi

In Delphi, virtual methods are marked with "virtual" keyword. Methods in descendant classes which override a virtual method in ancestor class are marked with "override" keyword. If a virtual method is defined in an ancestor class, but not defined in a descendant class, descendant class will use ancestor class' implementation of that method.

Delphi also provides another similar method type called; "Dynamic method". Dynamic methods are marked with "dynamic" keyword instead of "virtual" keyword. Dynamic methods in Delphi have the same functionality of Virtual methods, but Delphi compiler implements them differently. In general, Virtual methods have better performance than Dynamic methods. Here is an example of Virtual methods in Delphi:

```
{ Module 1: AnimalTypes.pas }

unit AnimalTypes;

interface

type
 Animal = class
 public
  procedure Eat; virtual;
 end;

 Wolf = class(Animal)
 public
  procedure Eat; override;
 end;

 Fish = class(Animal)
 public
  procedure Eat; override;
 end;

 GoldFish = class(Fish)
 public
  procedure Eat; override;
 end;

 OtherAnimal = class(Animal)
 public
  { Eat method is not overridden, so
the base class method will be used. }
 end;

implementation

{ Animal }
procedure Animal.Eat;
begin
 WriteLn('I eat like a generic Animal.
');
end;

{ Wolf }
procedure Wolf.Eat;
begin
 WriteLn('I eat like a wolf!');
end;

{ Fish }
procedure Fish.Eat;
begin
 WriteLn('I eat like a fish!');
end;

{ GoldFish }
```

```
procedure GoldFish.Eat;
begin
  WriteLn('I eat like a goldfish!');
end;

end.


{ Module 2: ConsoleApplication1.dpr }

program ConsoleApplication1;

{$APPTYPE CONSOLE}

uses
  Generics.Collections,
  AnimalTypes;

var
  Animals : TList<Animal>;
  CurrentAnimal : Animal;
begin
  Animals := TList<Animal>.Create;
  try
    Animals.Add(Animal.Create);
    Animals.Add(Wolf.Create);
    Animals.Add(Fish.Create);
    Animals.Add(GoldFish.Create);
    Animals.Add(OtherAnimal.Create);

    for CurrentAnimal in Animals do
      CurrentAnimal.Eat;
  finally
    Animals.Free;
  end;
end.
```

Output:

I eat like a generic Animal.
I eat like a wolf!
I eat like a fish!
I eat like a goldfish!
I eat like a generic Animal.

C#

In C#, a base class must provide the virtual modifier for any virtual method, and derived classes must provide the override modifier for any overridden method inherited from a base class. The following is an example in C#.NET

```
using System;
using System.Collections.Generic;

namespace ConsoleApplication1
{
 public class Animal
 {
  public virtual void Eat()
  {
   Console.WriteLine("I eat like a generic Animal.");
  }
 }

 public class Wolf : Animal
 {
  public override void Eat()
  {
   Console.WriteLine("I eat like a wolf!");
  }
 }

 public class Fish : Animal
 {
  public override void Eat()
  {
   Console.WriteLine("I eat like a fish!");
  }
 }

 public class GoldFish : Fish
 {
  public override void Eat()
  {
   Console.WriteLine("I eat like a goldfish!");
  }
 }

 public class OtherAnimal : Animal
 {
  // Eat() method is not overridden, so the base class method will be used.
 }

 public class Program
 {
  public static void Main(string[] args)
  {
   IList<Animal> animals = new List<Animal>();

   animals.Add(new Animal());
   animals.Add(new Wolf());
   animals.Add(new Fish());
   animals.Add(new GoldFish());
   animals.Add(new OtherAnimal());

   foreach (Animal currentAnimal in animals)
   {
    currentAnimal.Eat();
   }
  }
 }
}
```

Output:

I eat like a generic Animal.
I eat like a wolf!
I eat like a fish!
I eat like a goldfish!
I eat like a generic Animal.

VB.NET

In VB.NET, a base class must provide the Overridable modifier for any virtual method, and derived classes may provide the optional Overrides modifier for any overridden method inherited from a base class (this prevents a warning from being issued). The following is an example in VB.NET:

```
Imports System
Imports System.Collections.Generic

Namespace ConsoleApplication1

   Public Class Animal
      Public Overridable Sub Eat()
         Console.WriteLine("I eat like a
generic Animal.")
      End Sub
   End Class

   Public Class Wolf
      Inherits Animal
      Public Overrides Sub Eat()
         Console.WriteLine("I eat like a
wolf!")
      End Sub
   End Class

   Public Class Fish
      Inherits Animal
      Public Overrides Sub eat()
         Console.WriteLine("I eat like a
fish!")
      End Sub
   End Class

   Public Class Goldfish
      Inherits Fish
      Public Overrides Sub Eat()
         Console.WriteLine("I eat like a
goldfish!")
      End Sub
   End Class

   Public Class OtherAnimal
      Inherits Animal
      'Eat() method is not overridden,
so the base class method will be used.
   End Class

   Public Class Program
      Shared Sub Main()
         Dim animals As New List(Of
Animal)
         animals.Add(New Animal())
         animals.Add(New Wolf())
         animals.Add(New Fish())
         animals.Add(New Goldfish())
         animals.Add(New
OtherAnimal())

         For Each currentAnimal As
Animal In animals
            currentAnimal.Eat()
         Next
      End Sub
   End Class

End Namespace
```

Output:

```
I eat like a generic Animal.
I eat like a wolf!
I eat like a fish!
I eat like a goldfish!
I eat like a generic Animal.
```

Python

In Python all class functions (methods) are virtual.

```
class Animal:
   """Define an Animal base class"""
   def eat(self):
      """Class function (method) to
show how an Animal eats."""
      print "I eat like a generic Animal."

class Wolf(Animal):
   """Define a Wolf class (derived
from Animal)"""
   def eat(self):
      """Class function (method) to
show how a Wolf eats."""
      print "I eat like a wolf!"

class Fish(Animal):
   """Define a Fish class (derived from
Animal)"""
   def eat(self):
      """Class function (method) to
show how a Fish eats."""
      print "I eat like a fish!"

class GoldFish(Fish):
   """Define a GoldFish class (derived
from Fish)"""
   def eat(self):
      """Class function (method) to
show how a GoldFish eats."""
      print "I eat like a goldfish!"

class OtherAnimal(Animal):
   """Define an OtherAnimal class
(derived from Animal)"""
   ### eat() method is not overridden,
so the base class method will be used.

if __name__ == '__main__':
   ### Create a list of various animals.
   ### Could use a tuple intead of a list
if you wish.
   ### Could also create an empty list/
tuple and use the .append() class
function.
   animals = [ Animal(), Wolf(),
Fish(), GoldFish(), OtherAnimal() ]
   for a in animals:
      a.eat()
```

Output:

```
I eat like a generic Animal.
I eat like a wolf!
I eat like a fish!
I eat like a goldfish!
I eat like a generic Animal.
```

Ruby

In Ruby all instance methods are virtual.

```
class Animal
  def eat
    puts "I eat like a generic Animal."
  end
end

class Wolf < Animal
  def eat
    puts "I eat like a wolf!"
  end
end

class Fish < Animal
  def eat
    puts "I eat like a fish!"
  end
end

class GoldFish < Fish
  def eat
    puts "I eat like a goldfish!"
  end
end

class OtherAnimal < Animal
end

animals = [ Animal.new, Wolf.new, Fish.new, GoldFish.new, OtherAnimal.new ]
animals.each {|a| a.eat }
```

Output:

```
I eat like a generic Animal.
I eat like a wolf!
I eat like a fish!
I eat like a goldfish!
I eat like a generic Animal.
```

Abstract classes and pure virtual functions

A **pure virtual function** or **pure virtual method** is a virtual function that is required to be implemented by a derived class that is not abstract. Classes containing pure virtual methods are termed "abstract;" they cannot be instantiated directly, and a subclass of an abstract class can only be instantiated directly if all inherited pure virtual methods have been implemented by that class or a parent class. Pure virtual methods typically have a declaration (signature) and no definition (implementation).

As an example, an abstract base class "MathSymbol" may provide a pure virtual function doOperation(), and derived classes "Plus" and "Minus" implement doOperation() to provide concrete implementations. Implementing doOperation() would not make sense in the "MathSymbol" class as "MathSymbol" is an abstract concept whose behaviour is defined solely for each given kind (subclass) of "MathSymbol". Similarly, a given subclass of "MathSymbol" would not be complete without an implementation of doOperation().

Although pure virtual methods typically have no implementation in the class that declares them, pure virtual methods in C++ are permitted to contain an implementation in their declaring class, providing fallback or default behaviour that a derived class can delegate to if appropriate.

Pure virtual functions are also used where the method declarations are being used to define an interface for which derived classes will supply all implementations. An abstract class serving as an interface contains only pure virtual functions, and no data members or ordinary methods. Use of purely abstract classes as interfaces works in C++ as it supports multiple inheritance. Because many OO languages do not support multiple inheritance they often provide a separate interface mechanism. This is seen in Java for example.

C++

In C++, pure virtual functions are declared using a special syntax [= *0*] to set the function pointer to zero as demonstrated below.

```
class Abstract {
public:
  virtual void pure_virtual() = 0;
};
```

The pure virtual function declaration provides only the prototype of the method. Although an implementation of the pure virtual function is typically not provided in an abstract class, it may be included, although the definition may not be included at the point of declaration. Every non-abstract child class is still required to override the method, but the implementation provided by the abstract class may be called in this way:

```
void Abstract::pure_virtual() {
  // do something
}

class Child : public Abstract {
  virtual void pure_virtual(); // no
longer abstract, this class may be
                    // instantiated.
};

void Child::pure_virtual() {
  Abstract::pure_virtual(); // the
implementation in the abstract class
                   // is executed
}
```

Java and C#

In Java and C#, pure virtual methods are declared using the *abstract* keyword. Such a method cannot have a body. A class containing abstract methods (either directly, or inherited and not overridden) must itself be declared abstract. (But the converse is not true - an abstract class is not required to have any abstract methods.) An abstract class cannot be instantiated. Any concrete (instantiable) class with an abstract class as its ancestor must implement all unimplemented abstract methods in order to successfully compile.

```
abstract class B {
   abstract void a_pure_virtual
_function();
}
```

Java and C# also use interfaces. All of the methods declared in an interface are implicitly abstract:

```
interface C {
   void a_pure_virtual_function();
}
```

VB.NET

In VB.NET, pure virtual function may be declared using MustOverride keyword, which would make the class not instantiatable. If another class inherits it, it must provide an overriding method (using "Overrides" keyword, see above) in order to be instantiatable. Note that 'End Sub'/'End Function'/'End Property' statement is not needed for pure virtual functions in VB.NET.

```
Public Class Animal
   Public MustOverride Sub Eat()
End Class
```

Just like Java and C#, an interface may be used instead:

```
Public Interface Animal
   Public Sub Eat()
End Interface
```

Behaviour during construction and destruction

Languages differ in their behaviour while the constructor or destructor of an object is running. For some languages, notably C++, the virtual dispatching mechanism has different semantics during construction and destruction of an object. While it is recommended that virtual function calls in constructors should be avoided for C++, in some other languages, for example Java and C#, the derived implementation can be called during construction and design patterns such as the Abstract Factory Pattern actively promote this usage in languages supporting the ability.

C++

```
#include <iostream>
#include <string>

using namespace std;

struct A
{
 virtual string name() const { return
"A"; }
 virtual ~A() { cout << "Destructing "
<< name() << endl; }
};

struct B : A
{
 B() { cout << "Constructing " <<
name() << endl; }
 virtual string name() const { return
"B"; }
};

struct C : B
{
 virtual string name() const { return
"C"; }
};

int main()
{
 C c; // Output: "Constructing B"

} // Output: "Destructing A"
```

Java

```
public class Base {
 public int length() {
  return 0;
 }

 public Base() {
  System.out.println("Constructing "
+ length());
 }

 static class Derived extends Base {
  String name;
  public Derived(String name) {
   this.name = (name != null) ? name
: ""; // Class invariant this.name is not
null
  }
  public int length() {
   return name.length(); // Assume
name is not null
  }
 }

 public static void  main(String[] args)
{
  new Derived("Ooops");   //
NullPointerException, Derived.name
has not been assigned to yet
 }
}
```

This is because the constructor of Base is executed before the constructor of Derived. As the constructor of Base calls length(), a null pointer exception is thrown.

Virtual destructors

Object-oriented languages typically manage memory allocation and deallocation automatically when objects are created and destroyed, however some object-oriented languages allow a custom destructor method to be implemented if desired. One such language is C++, and as illustrated in the following example, it is important for a C++ base class to have a virtual destructor to ensure that the destructor from the most derived class will always be called.

In the example below having no virtual destructor, while deleting an instance of class B will correctly call destructors for both B and A if the object is deleted as an instance of B, an instance of B deleted via a pointer to its base class A will produce undefined behaviour. On many implementations, the destructor for B will not be called in this situation.

```
#include <iostream>
using namespace std;

class A
{
public:

  A() { }
  ~A() { cout << "Destroy A" << endl;
}
};

class B : public A
{
public:

  B() { }
  ~B() { cout << "Destroy B" << endl;
}
};

int main()
{
  A* b1 = new B;
  B* b2 = new B;

  delete b1; // According to the C++
standard,
          // the behaviour of this is
undefined.
          // Usually, only ~A() is called
though b1 is an instance
          // of class B because ~A() is
not declared virtual.
  delete b2; // Calls destructors ~B()
and ~A()

  return 0;
}
```

Possible output:

Destroy A
Destroy B
Destroy A

Correctly declaring the destructor for class A as virtual ~A() will ensure that the destructor for class B is called in both cases with the example above.
Source (edited): "http://en.wikipedia.org/wiki/Virtual_function"

Virtual inheritance

For inheritance of virtual functions, see virtual function.

Virtual inheritance is a topic of object-oriented programming. It is a kind of inheritance in which the part of the object that belongs to the **virtual base** class becomes common direct base for the derived class and any next class that derives from it. In other words, if class *A* is virtually derived from class *V*, and class *B* is derived (directly or indirectly) from *A*, then *V* becomes a direct base class of class *B* and any other class derived from *A*. The best known language that is known to implement this feature is C++.

This feature is most useful for multiple inheritance, as it causes that subobject (it could be said "instance", stating that *V* isn't abstract) of the virtual base will be always a common subobject for all classes that are derived in the deriving class (as well as this class itself). This can be used to avoid the problem of ambiguous hierarchy composition (known as the "diamond problem") by clarifying ambiguity over which ancestor class to use, as from the perspective of the deriving class (*B* in the example above) the virtual base (*V*) looks as if it was its direct base class, not a class being derived indirectly through its bases (*A*). This way, such a hierarchy doesn't form a diamond.

It is used when inheritance is representing restrictions of a set rather than composition of parts. In C++, a base class to be common in the hierarchy is denoted as virtual with the virtual keyword.

The problem

Consider the following class hierarchy.

```
class Animal
{
 public:
  virtual void eat();
};

class Mammal : public Animal
{
 public:
  virtual void walk();
};

class WingedAnimal : public Animal
{
 public:
  virtual void flap();
};

// A bat is a winged mammal
class Bat : public Mammal, public
WingedAnimal {};

Bat bat;
```

As declared above, a call to bat.eat() is ambiguous. The ambiguity is caused by the way C++ implementations typically represent classes. In particular, inheritance is simply a matter of putting parent and child classes one after the other in memory. Thus, Bat is represented as (Animal, Mammal, Animal, WingedAnimal, Bat), which makes Animal duplicated (in other words, Bat owns *two different* Animal instances, namely a Mammal::Animal and a WingedAnimal::Animal). To disambiguate, one would have to explicitly call either bat.Mammal::eat() or bat. WingedAnimal::eat().

Similarly, an attempt to directly cast a Bat object to an Animal would fail, since the cast is ambiguous.

```
Animal a = (Animal)Bat(); //error:
which Animal instance should a Bat
cast into,
                    //a Mammal::Animal
or a WingedAnimal::Animal?
```

As noted, the code would fail to compile, despite the fact that the two different Animals are 'identical' (for example, no virtual members of Animal are being overridden by Mammal or WingedAnimal). To fix the code without using virtual inheritance, it would be necessary to first cast to one of the two inherited classes and then make the cast to Animal.

```
Animal a = (Animal)(Mammal)Bat();
//ok: compiler chooses
Mammal::Animal after
                    //cast to Mammal
```

This situation is sometimes referred to as **diamond inheritance** (see Diamond problem) because the inheritance diagram is in the shape of a diamond. Virtual inheritance can help to solve this problem.

The solution

We can re-declare our classes as follows:

```
class Animal
{
 public:
  virtual void eat();
};

// Two classes virtually inheriting
Animal:
class Mammal : public virtual Animal
{
 public:
  virtual void walk();
};

class WingedAnimal : public virtual
Animal
{
 public:
  virtual void flap();
};

// A bat is still a winged mammal
class Bat : public Mammal, public
WingedAnimal {};
```

The Animal portion of Bat::WingedAnimal is now the *same* Animal instance as the one used by Bat::Mammal, which is to say that a Bat has only one, shared, Animal instance in its representation and so a call to Bat::eat() is unambiguous. Additionally, a direct cast from Bat to Animal is also unambiguous, now that there exists only one Animal instance which Bat could be converted to.

This is implemented by providing Mammal and WingedAnimal with a vtable pointer (or "vpointer") since the memory offset between the beginning of a Mammal and of its Animal part is unknown until runtime. Thus Bat becomes (vpointer, Mammal, vpointer, WingedAnimal, Bat, Animal). There are two vtable pointers, one per inheritance hierarchy that virtually inherits Animal. In this example, one for Mammal and one for WingedAnimal. The object size has therefore increased by two pointers, but now there is only one Animal and no ambiguity. All objects of type Bat will have the same vpointers, but each Bat object will contain its own unique Animal object. If another class inherits from Mammal, such as Squirrel, then the vpointer in the

Mammal object in a Squirrel will be different from the vpointer in the Mammal object in a Bat, although they can still be essentially the same in the special case that the Squirrel part of the object has the same size as the Bat part, because then the distance from the Mammal to the Animal part is the same. The vtables are not really the same, but all essential information in them (the distance) is.

Source (edited): "http://en.wikipedia.org/wiki/Virtual_inheritance"

Wide character

A **wide character** is a computer character datatype that generally has a size greater than the traditional 8-bit character. The increased datatype size allows for the use of larger coded character sets.

History

During the 1960s, mainframe and mini-computer manufacturers began to standardize around the 8-bit byte as their smallest datatype. Meanwhile, the 7-bit ASCII character set became the industry standard method for encoding alphanumeric characters for teletype machines and computer terminals. As a result, the 8-bit byte became the de facto datatype for computer systems storing ASCII characters in memory.

Later, computer manufacturers began to make use of the spare bit to extend the ASCII character set beyond its limited set of English alphabet characters. 8-bit extensions such as IBM code page 37, PETSCII and ISO 8859 became commonplace, offering terminal support for Greek, Cyrillic, and many others. However, such extensions were still limited in that they were region specific and often could not be used in tandem. Special conversion routines had to be used to convert from one character set to another, often resulting in destructive translation when no equivalent character existed in the target set.

In 1989, the International Organization for Standardization began work on the Universal Character Set (UCS), a multilingual character set that could be encoded using either a 16-bit (2-byte) or 32-bit (4-byte) value. These larger values required the use of a datatype larger than 8-bits to store the new character values in memory. Thus the term wide character was used to differentiate them from traditional 8-bit character datatypes.

Relation to UCS and Unicode

A wide character refers to the size of the datatype in memory. It does not state how each value in a character set is defined. Those values are instead defined using character sets, with UCS and Unicode simply being two common character sets that contain more characters than an 8-bit value would allow.

Relation to multibyte characters

Just as earlier data transmission systems suffered from the lack of an 8-bit clean data path, modern transmission systems often lack support for 16-bit or 32-bit data paths for character data. This has led to character encoding systems such as UTF-8 that can use multiple bytes to encode a value that is too large for a single 8-bit symbol.

Size of a wide character

The Microsoft Windows application programming interfaces Win32 and Win64, as well as the Java and .Net Framework platforms, require that wide character variables be defined as 16-bit values, and that characters be encoded using UTF-16 (due to former use of UCS-2), while modern Unix-like systems generally require 32-bit values encoded using UTF-32.

Programming specifics

C/C++

The ISO/IEC C programming language, which generally uses the datatype wchar_t for wide characters, originally defined that wide characters should be 16-bit values under C90 due to historical compatibility reasons. C and C++ compilers that comply with the 10646-1:2000 Unicode standard generally assume 32-bit values. However, the ISO/IEC 10646:2003 Unicode standard 4.0 says that:

"ANSI/ISO C leaves the semantics of the wide character set to the specific implementation but requires that the characters from the portable C execution set correspond to their wide character equivalents by zero extension."

and that

"The width of wchar_t is compiler-specific and can be as small as 8 bits. Consequently, programs that need to be portable across any C or C++ compiler should not use wchar_t for storing Unicode text. The wchar_t type is intended for storing compiler-defined wide characters, which may be Unicode characters in some compilers."

In ANSI C library header files, wchar.h and wctype.h deal with the wide characters. Additional functions can also be found in stdio.h and stdlib.h.

Wide characters and long strings must use the prefix **L** when defined in quotes. Some examples are:

```
wchar_t myChar1 = L'Ω';
wchar_t myChar2 = 0x2126; //
hexadecimal encoding of char Ω using
UTF-16
wchar_t myString1[] = L"♠♣♥♦";
wchar_t myString2[] = { 0x2660,
0x2661, 0x2662, 0x2663, 0x0000 };
// hex encoding of null-terminated
string ♠♣♥♦ using UTF-16

printf("This is a long string: %ls
\n",myString1);
wprintf(L"This is a long string: %s
\n",myString2);
```

Python

According to Python's documentation, the language sometimes uses wchar_t as the basis for its character type Py_UNICODE. It depends on whether wchar_t is "compatible with the chosen Python Unicode build variant" on that system. Source (edited): "http://en.wikipedia. org/wiki/Wide_character"